FAMILY GROWTH

ELECTIVES

Raising Kids in a Violent Culture

Studies for Today's Parents

Mike Murphy and Victoria Johnson

David C. Cook Publishing Co., Elgin, Illinois—Paris, Ontario

Raising Kids in a Violent Culture
© 1995 David C. Cook Publishing Co.

850 N. Grove Ave., Elgin, IL 60120-2892
Cable address: DCCOOK
Cover designers: Tom Schild and Jack Foster
Cover illustrator: Pete Whyte
Illustrator: Guy Wolek
Product Developer: Terri Hibbard
Editors: Dave and Neta Jackson
Printed in U.S.A.

ISBN: 0-7814-5139-6

1   2   3   4   5   6   7   8   9   10

Contents

Welcome to Family Growth Electives

Congratulations! The fact that you are using a study in the Family Growth Electives series says that you are concerned about today's families. You and your group of parents are about to begin an exciting adventure.

Each course in this series has been created with today's families in mind. Rather than taking a single topic and applying it to all adults, these Family Growth Electives treat each adult life stage or situation separately. This means that people who are approaching or going through similar stages in life can get together to share and study their common needs from a biblical perspective.

The concept of family life stages comes from the work of Dr. Dennis B. Guernsey, associate professor of Marital and Family Therapy, Fuller Theological Seminary. Guernsey says that the family has critical tasks to accomplish at each stage in order to nurture healthy Christians.

Many adults in churches today have not come from strong Christian roots. Others may have attended church as children, drifted away during their adolescent or young adult years, and are now back in church in an effort to get help with the everyday problems of family life.

Some adults do not have the benefits of living near their extended family. The church can meet the needs of such people by becoming their "family." It can also help strengthen families by teaching them biblical principles and giving opportunities for applying those principles. That's exactly what you'll be doing as you lead your group in this Family Growth Electives study.

Dave and Neta Jackson, Editors

Introduction

This course is for parents who know that the environment in which their children live is too violent. It may be the violence of the media, the toys with which their children play, or the schools and streets through which they must move. Whatever the source, it is a cause for major concern.

The *U.S. News and World Report* recently estimated that more than three million crimes a year are committed in or near the eighty-five thousand U.S. public schools. A University of Michigan study reported that 9 percent of eighth-graders carry a gun, knife, or club to school at least once a month. In all, an estimated 270,000 guns go to school every day. Twenty percent of suburban high schoolers surveyed by Tulane University researchers thought it was appropriate to shoot someone "who has stolen something from you." Eight percent believed it is all right to shoot a person who had "done something to offend or insult you."[1]

A generation ago, white families used to flee to the suburbs to escape what frightened them about the city. Many ethnic families do not have that option. But even if it were available, it would be small comfort. Today, while you can run, you cannot hide! While big cities may still have the greatest number of kids involved in gangs, the largest *growth* of gang activity today is occurring in small towns and rural areas.

So how can the children of the parents in your group survive and even thrive in our violent society?

In this course, your group members will gain a biblical perspective and learn many helpful tips about how families can cope with the violence in the society around them as they participate in the active learning in this course. You'll find activities for group members to do alone, as couples, in small groups, and with the entire group together.

As the leader, you will find this course easy to prepare and easy to use. You do not have to be an expert yourself. Each forty-five- to sixty-minute session includes step-by-step instructions printed in regular type. Each session begins with "Getting Ready" which lists everything you need to do before group time. To help you pace yourself according to your available time, there are suggested time frames for each step.

All content is Scripture-based. At the beginning of each session plan you will find a list of the Scriptures to be covered.

Things you might say aloud to your group are in **bold type**. Of course, it is always best to restate things in your own words. Suggested answers to questions are in parentheses.

Each of the thirteen sessions has reproducible resource sheets. In most cases you will use these as handouts for group members. It would also work to turn some resources into overhead transparencies if you'd like.

Raising Kids in a Violent Culture can be a source of encouragement and growth for your group members. By using this Family Growth Elective, you will nurture growth in the lives of your adults—growth in their relationships with the Lord, each other, and their children.

1. Thomas Toch, "Violence in the Schools," *U.S. News and World Report*, Nov. 8, 1993, 31-35, as reported in *Focus on the Family* newsletter, Jan. 1994, 5.

When I Was Your Age . . .

1

Session Aim:
To have parents examine their own "growing up" and the role violence played then compared to now; to identify sin as the root cause of violence.

When I was your age, we didn't look like punks. People weren't shooting one another. We weren't afraid to walk outside like we are today."

Sound familiar? What was it *really* like when you were growing up? Was violence around then?

I remember walking into a rival school pep rally and being chased for several blocks by some pretty scary "greasers." I lived in a town of only thirty-five thousand people, but there was a section we stayed away from after dark. Guys fought over girls and calls in football games. Alcohol abuse and the violence that accompanies it happened then too. A classmate's brother was killed on his morning paper route. Growing up was fine, but life wasn't always as portrayed in a 1950s' sitcom.

Violence is not new. Sometimes we tend to think that it is. It is part of having a selective memory. Violence is nothing more than a horrible expression of sin, and we all know how long sin's been with us. Our culture has changed, the amount and frequency of violence has increased, and the changes are pretty scary. In some cities and towns crossing boundaries into another neighborhood might mean more than a chase. It could mean gunfire, possibly even death. It is time to face up to what was and what is so we can deal effectively with this more violent society in which we find ourselves.

—*Mike Murphy*

*I*t is important for the parents to acknowledge that violence was present when they were young. . . .

Getting Ready

Scriptures:
Genesis 4:1-13; Galatians 5:19-21; James 4:1-7.

1. Make one photocopy of "Memory Ticklers" (RS-1A), and cut up the sheet into individual "ticklers." Place these into a hat for distribution to the group members.
2. Photocopy enough copies of "Violence: Then and Now" (RS-1B) for everyone in the group.
3. Photocopy more than enough copies of "Too Much Violence" (RS-1C) for every parent so that those parents who are interested in surveying more than one child can do so.
4. Be sure to have extra paper for those who might need it.

❶ Was I Ever Young?

Objective:
To give parents an opportunity to get to know each other and to reflect on their growing up years (15 minutes).

As a warm-up have parents introduce themselves, share the ages of their children, and briefly state why they decided to attend this group. Pass the hat with "Memory Ticklers" (RS-1A). Have everyone take a "tickler" and respond based on personal experiences as a child or adolescent.

For this activity, it is more fun if people can try to remember what was happening when they were in either junior or senior high. If someone feels uncomfortable with the "tickler" he or she has drawn, allow that person to pick a new one. Have fun with this. It is okay if people "hitchhike" off of what someone else says and describes, for instance, their own memories of their favorite hangouts even though that slip was drawn by someone else.

After everyone shares, ask the participants what they see as the biggest difference between growing up in today's world as compared to the world they grew up in. Jot down general observations on the board.

❷ Violence: Is It Really Worse Now?

Objective:
To have group members explore their perceptions of the levels of violence present today as compared to when they were growing up (15 minutes).

Focus the discussion on the issue of violence by distributing copies of "Violence: Then and Now" (RS-1B). Have participants spend a few moments filling out the worksheet. Have them jot notes in each box that will help them remember their impressions for the subsequent discussion. Details are not important.

You might need to help people reflect on the nature of violence when they were growing up. For instance, you can prime the pump by reading the remarks in the introduction or by introducing your own thoughts. It is important for the parents to acknowledge that violence was present when they were young, though they may have felt very sheltered from its reality.

Do not be afraid to give them hints. For instance, even in a story as benign as *The Sound of Music* there was the underlying horror of the Third Reich and an imminent threat of violence to the Von Trapp family, and *West Side Story* portrayed a violent though glamorized (by music and dance) interpretation of gang life.

Early rock 'n' roll may have seemed like nothing but fun and games at the time, but it was born out of rhythm and blues, a musical tradition that expressed great pain. Even at the time, rock 'n' roll was considered by many adults as the ultimate sign of rebellion.

"The Untouchables" was a prime-time television favorite and the nightly news brought us the violence of the Civil Rights Movement, the Vietnam War, the '68 National Democratic Convention, the assassination of national leaders, and widespread rioting.

And what school child hasn't witnessed a playground fight or street fight at one time or another?

It is possible people won't remember some things. That's okay. Our culture was at a different place years ago. The theme of violence didn't capture people's attention and fears the way it does today.

Explore the ways they think our society has changed: **What have been some of the big changes that have occurred since we were kids? How have these changes impacted our culture? Have these contributed in any way to the development of a more violent society?** Allow a few moments for response. Do not try to get parents to offer specific answers. Even no answer is okay. This is only to get them thinking.

Gordon McLean, in *Cities of Lonesome Fear: God Among the Gangs*, **identifies four major changes which have affected our children.** List and number the underlined phrases on the board as you come to them.

When kids seem to be spinning out of control, some parents try to regain their footing by recalling, "Back when I was your age . . ." But few, if any, contemporary adults ever lived in an age such as this. Not many of us grew up going to school where violence was a fact of daily life and coke (the

illegal drug) was easier to get than a Coke [the carbonated drink].

The enormous changes that have created this different world did not happen overnight. By talking with parents about how it was when they were young, we see patterns of change emerging.

• First, kids lost their innocence when television became a staple in the home, presenting lifestyles that are alien and offensive to traditional families as normal and acceptable.

• Then kids lost their respect for social mores (beliefs, customs, traditions, manners) as the drug culture offered the challenge to "tune in, turn on, and drop out."

• Next, kids lost their values as intellectuals proclaimed, "God is dead," and everything sacred was up for grabs.

• Finally, kids have lost their hope. This is the first generation that does not see itself living better than its parents, a sure sign of the impact of worldwide economic and social upheaval. "So why get an education?" many young people ask. "Nobody's going anywhere." The key words for many urban kids in the nineties are alone, fear, despair.[1]

Generate discussion with these comments and questions:

Name some negative behaviors that are often portrayed on television as normal and acceptable. (Premarital sex, defiant talk to parents, drinking at teen parties, and disrespect for authority.)

In what ways did the drug culture challenge traditional mores? (Insobriety is cool. Hard work is foolish. The "establishment" is something to scorn, not join and improve.)

What attitudes result when society abandons its common belief in God? (Common standards of right and wrong disappear. Purpose in living is eroded. Motivation to serve others is diminished.)

How have modern kids lost hope? (If life is meaningless, there is no reason to try and do better in any area.)

❸ Could Sin Be the Problem?

Objective:
To identify sin as the root cause of violence (10 minutes).

Have the people open their Bibles. Ask for volunteers to read the following Scriptures. After each one, encourage discussion on the source of violence by asking the suggested questions.

Genesis 4:1-13

What was the source of Cain's hatred of his brother? (He was jealous and angry that God did not look with favor on his offering like He did on Abel's sacrifice. Some respondents may suggest that Cain disobeyed God by trying to bring a vegetable offering when God desired a blood sacrifice. God had provided that example by preparing skin clothes to cover the nakedness of Adam and Eve's sin [see Gen. 3:21], but there is no record that God had previously made that a requirement for an acceptable sacrifice. At the very least, Cain refused to be corrected.)

What are the implications for society if people accept or adopt Cain's attitude, "Am I my brother's keeper"? (It is always God's intention that we live in community, caring for one another. The attitude that we don't need to do this breeds and encourages violence.)

Galatians 5:19-21

What are the consequences for those who persist in or defend sinful behaviors? (They "will not inherit the kingdom of God.")

James 4:1-7

The King James Version asks, "From whence come wars and fightings among you?" How would you answer this question? (The passage identifies sin as the source, but let the group personalize this in regard to the violence about which they are concerned.)

Summarize the Bible study by making the point that "violence" is a symptom of a spiritual problem. It is a direct consequence of sin. Discuss: **How accurate is this ancient record—the Bible—to our world today?** If you have nonbelievers in your group, this may be a good opportunity to identify and discuss the Bible as God's reliable Word to us.

Our culture has changed, the amount and frequency of violence has increased, and the changes are pretty scary.

❹ What Do Your Kids Have to Say about Violence?

Objective:

To encourage parents to discuss with their children common forms of violence in their schools and neighborhoods and to have parents express one way they hope this course will help them. (5-20 minutes).

Distribute copies of "Too Much Violence" (RS-1C), encouraging those who wish to survey more than one child to take extra copies. Urge the participants to explore the topic of violence with their own children by using the questionnaire. Older children can fill out the form on their own. Parents can administer the questionnaire to younger children.

Explain that this questionnaire can be very useful in helping parents dialog with their children. Dialog is a skill that needs to be in every parents tool box for effective parenting. Caution the parents that this should not be a time for scolding or arguing with their children. They are trying to explore their kids' perceptions about violence, not evaluate their friends.

Tell the parents that they should bring the completed questionnaire back to the next session. Not only are we trying to get information from the children in this survey but we are trying to provide a way of talking about a very important issue. So, encourage parents to follow-through with this exercise.

Once you have passed out the questionnaire, share the following information compiled from *Youth Worker Update* to give the parents a realistic perspective.

- One in five females has been a victim of sexual assault, in most cases by someone she knew. In a third of the cases, the assailant was another student.
- One in three know someone who has brought a weapon to school.
- Forty-two percent of the males have access to one or more firearms.
- More than half reported frequent fights between students.
- Five percent said there had been a shooting on school grounds, and 7 percent reported a knife fight.
- Seventeen percent reported that a teacher in their school had been assaulted.
- One-third considered suicide.[2]

To close this session, have the parents use the back of either RS-1A or RS-1B to complete this statement. "I hope this course will help me . . ." Encourage the group members to keep this statement for evaluation at the end of the course.

If you have a full hour for group time, invite the parents to share their statements with the whole group and report on their own experiences or concerns about violence. Begin by asking for volunteers, rather than going around the circle as

Close by praying for several of the needs expressed in the sharing time.

sharing may be an emotional thing for some. Maybe their child has been involved in violence or threatened at school or in the neighborhood. Maybe drug activity is going on in their neighborhood. Some may even have "lost" a child to a gang, prison, or even death. If the group is developing a warm and safe environment, you might invite "holdouts" to share near the end, but don't pressure people.

Close by praying for several of the needs expressed in the sharing time. If you did not have time for the final sharing, pray for the group's experience and the general needs of our children.

Remind parents to bring their completed surveys for next session.

Notes:

1. Gordon McLean with Dave and Neta Jackson, *Cities of Lonesome Fear: God Among the Gangs* (Chicago: Moody Press, 1991), 66, 67. Underlining added.

2. Compiled from *Youth Worker Update*, Newsletter for Christian Youth Workers, December 1993, 5.

You Can Run, But You Can't Hide

2

Session Aim:
To examine the impact of violence on children and adults.

Those who live in the suburbs of Chicago have a saying, "When Chicago coughs, we catch a cold." But is that how violence spreads? Suburbanites often think all violence originates in low-income, inner-city neighborhoods and spills over into the nice, peaceful suburban and rural areas. This is not true. Violence has no boundaries.

I live in a suburban town of seventy-five thousand people. In the past six months two teenagers have been killed within two blocks of my home. A young man who is in my Young Life Club was killed in a drive-by shooting. My son had a toy gun put to his head during a playground incident. It looked so real that he came home quite shaken.

A friend moved away from the city to an affluent area to get his daughter away from urban gang activity. Within one week she was befriended by "gangbangers." Now my friend wants to know, "Is there any place we can go to escape?"

We visited a family in a mid-size, rural town in Wisconsin. The morning newspaper featured an article entitled, "The Growing Threat of Gang Violence." The article estimated that over two hundred local young people were involved in gangs.

Many people are choosing violence as a primary means of interacting with each other. The impact of those choices are far-reaching and in some ways, very scary.

—*Mike Murphy*

Many people are choosing violence as a primary means of interacting with each other.

Getting Ready

Scriptures:
Romans 1:18-32; II Timothy 3:1-5; Mark 9:33-37; 10:13-16.

1. Make photocopies of "Survey Result Questions" (RS-2A), "Listen to the Children" (RS-2B), and "Parents Look at Violence" (RS-2C), for everyone in the class.
2. For the "Violence Continuum" in Step 1 make two signs: "Violence: No Impact (1)" and "Violence: Big Impact (10)." Arrange the room according to the instructions in Step 1.
3. Bring newspaper clippings of violent incidents from your local newspaper.
4. Optional: a tape player and cassette with soft instrumental music.
5. Be sure you have completed the survey from last week, "Too Much Violence" (RS-1C) with several kids so you can offer results in Step 3 of this session.

❶ Violence Impacts Us All

Objective:
To focus attention on the reality of violence in our midst (10-15 minutes).

Begin the session by having the group create a living "Violence Continuum" as explained below:

Clear a large space in your room. At one end place a chair with a sign on it reading, "Violence: No Impact (1)." At the other end of the space, place a chair with a sign on it reading, "Violence: Big Impact (10)." Explain to the group that as you announce various things that violence impacts, they should arrange themselves between the two signs as though they were standing on a continuum where their position represents their opinion from "1"(no impact) to "10" (big impact).

After you read each statement and the parents have taken their positions, have them take turns sharing why they are standing where they are. If your group is large, you may want them to share only with the person nearest them so that the sharing will not take so long.

a. Impact of violence on our culture
b. Impact of violence on your kids
c. Impact of violence on you personally
d. Impact of violence on your neighborhood

Have the parents help you rearrange the chairs and take their seats. Then read the statement by Mike Murphy that introduces this session. Stimulate a brief discussion by asking the group: **Can you recall any examples of violence that have occurred recently in your community?** Have local newspaper clippings ready as examples if group does not quickly offer examples. List all examples on the board.

This generation is in need of a resurrection and the new life Jesus Christ offers.

❷ Getting to the Root of the Problem

Objective:
To reinforce the concept of "sin" as the root cause of violence (15 minutes).

In Session 1 the root cause of evil and violence was identified as sin. (Scriptures from Session 1: Genesis 4:1-13—jealousy, anger, and the lack of caring motivated Cain to murder Abel. Galatians 5:19-21—the hatred, discord, jealousy, and rage that come from the sinful nature cannot be part of the kingdom of God. James 4:1-7—the source of conflict is selfishness.) But this root cause is not acknowledged by many secular analysts.

Ask the group to discuss: **What do you think secular analysts such as many counselors, teachers, or politicians point to as the problem for violence in our society?** Allow the group to freely offer their opinions, then read a quote from *Cities of Lonesome Fear: God Among the Gangs* by Gordon McLean, the director of the juvenile justice ministry of Metro Chicago Youth for Christ.

> **When secular analysts look at problems, they tend to focus on the symptoms rather than causes. Listen to the observation of a group of counselors.**
> • **"The home, school, and church used to act as a restraint on youthful behavior."**
> • **"There is usually just a mother alone raising a family."**
> • **"Some parents use alcohol themselves."**
> • **"Parents attack each other."**
> • **"There is no one for kids to talk to."**[1]

These statements describe what many considered are the causes of a generation gone wild. But, from a Christian perspective, they describe symptoms of a spiritually dead generation. This generation is in need of a resurrection and the new life Jesus Christ offers.

Ask: **What are some of the solutions commonly given for the violence problem?** (Stabilize the school system, more money for community programs, eliminate racism, more jobs, better law enforcement system, death penalty, etc.)

It is true, educational inequalities, lack of family stability, employment issues, racism, etc., contribute to the development of a violent culture. Christians need to be involved, helping to resolve these important issues. God cares deeply about anyone feeling the "sting of sin," and so should we.

However, a trap we need to avoid is assuming that

exploitation, violence, racism, etc. will disappear if and when secular solutions are implemented. The problem is deeper than surface solutions. It's a sinful heart problem. Sin creates trouble. When the spiritual dimension is neglected, we start to believe in human abilities and to solve problems by leaning on self, not God. Too often spiritual strategies become secondary instead of primary resources.

Break the class into two groups. Assign one group to study Romans 1:18-32 and the other group to study II Timothy 3:1-5. Have them identify the sins mentioned in their respective passages, noting in which verse(s) the sin is mentioned. Have one person in each group record the findings.

While the groups are working on the Scripture passages, prepare the chalk or marker board with two headings: on the left, "Violent Activities," and on the right, "Sins Identified in Scripture." Spaced several "lines" apart under the left heading list these acts: Rapes, Muggings, Murders, Beatings.

When you reconvene the group, ask the teams to report on the sins they found in the passages. When a sin is listed, ask the group: **To which violent act might that sin lead?** Record their responses accordingly on the board. It may look like this with the italicized entries being the group's contributions:

Violent Activities	Sins (Attitudes or Actions) Identified in Scripture
Rapes	*Romans 1:18, 24—Godlessness, impurity* *II Timothy 3:2, 3—Abusive, without self-control, brutal, unholy*
Muggings	*Romans 1:25, 29—Serve the creature rather than the Creator, greed* *II Timothy 3:2—Lovers of self and money*
Murders	*Romans 1:28—Depraved minds* *II Timothy 3:3, 4—Without love, treacherous*
Beatings	*Romans 1:31—Heartless, ruthless* *II Timothy 3:3, 4—Brutal and rash*

Have someone read Romans 1:24, 25. **According to these verses, why do people get involved in violent activities?**

Too often we look at the symptoms of sin as the issue rather than sin itself.

("God gave them over in the sinful desires of their hearts." God allowed their sinful appetites to take control. "They exchanged the truth of God for a lie, and worshipped and served created things rather than the Creator." People are naturally more interested in things rather than God.)

In what ways is sin like a cancer? (Both claim victims. Sometimes the victims are obvious: a person is shot, a woman raped, a child abused, or a leg is lost, surgery is required, strength is lost. Both can also spread—initially, at least—without any indication. Potential victims see their freedom limited because of fear: it affects the mind, generates doubt, raises barriers between people, etc. Both start small and continue to grow until they affect wide area, incapacitating the victims.)

Why is it important to identify sin as the root cause of violence? (If a person with cancer only tries to treat the pain, he or she will not be cured. We want to treat the true disease, not merely the symptoms. As Christians, we must always look at the spiritual dimension of any problem we face. That is our starting point in discussing the issues. Too often we look at the symptoms of sin as the issue rather than sin itself.)

❸ Kids Say the Saddest Things

Objective:
To discuss the response of children toward violence (10-15 minutes).

Pass out "Survey Result Questions" (RS-2A) and "Listen to the Children" (RS-2B). Break the participants into groups of three or four to work on the sheets. Make sure at least one person in each group has a completed survey. Have them follow the instructions on both work sheets. If you completed surveys with kids, you could share your results at this point. If no one in the group was able to complete the survey, move on to "Listen to the Children."

Bring the group back together and read Mark 9:33-37 and 10:13-16. (Option: If you have a cassette player, play soft, instrumental music in the background as you read.) Have a time of silent prayer for the young people caught in frightening situations. Then, ask someone to pray out loud about the violence we see, the victims, and the perpetrators.

❹ The Impact of Violence on Us

Objective:
To give parents the opportunity to talk about how violence impacts them (10-15 minutes).

Pass out "Parents Look at Violence" (RS-2C). Give the parents a few minutes to fill out the questionnaire, then discuss the questions. Try to capture the mood of the group towards violence.

Try to be reassuring and hopeful that the course will attempt to tackle some of these difficult questions and come up with solutions.

Encourage parents to continue talking with their children. Ask the parents to read the work sheet "Listen to the Children" (RS-2B) with their kids. If the children are small, the parents could ask them to draw a picture of their neighborhood. Suggest that they encourage discussion with their children by asking: **What is happening to these children in the article? Why do they feel so frightened? Do you have similar feelings about your neighborhood? Tell me about your picture.**

Close the session by encouraging the parents that in future sessions, more responses and solutions will be suggested. Pray that God will give group members His perspective on violence, solutions to the related problems, and a sense of hope.

Notes:

1. Gordon McLean with Dave and Neta Jackson, *Cities of Lonesome Fear: God Among the Gangs* (Chicago: Moody Press, 1991), 76, 77.

How Did We Get Where We Are?

3

Session Aim:
To identify cultural messages that contribute to a violent climate and explore the impact of those messages on adults.

Did you know there is a war being waged?

During the next two sessions we will be looking at a battleground. The battle is for our minds and the minds our children. The enemy is very real. The weapon Satan uses is a seductive, philosophical world view. He attempts to snare people into believing that there is no such thing as right or wrong, that moral absolutes are for the weak, and that God is not relevant today.

Christian or not, parents need to be aware of the competing philosophies that are trying to lure them and their kids into some dangerous turf. That turf is fertile ground for drugs, sexual immorality, and violence. We live in an "anything goes" world.

In contrast, the Bible gives the Christian world view. In the J. B. Phillips translation Ephesians 1:9-11 says, "For God has allowed us to know the secret of his plan, it is this: he purposes in his sovereign will that all human history shall be consummated in Christ, that everything that exists in Heaven or earth shall find its perfection and fulfillment in him."

Pretty clearly laid out, don't you think? On one side you have a group urging people to find fulfillment in just about anything but God and His Word. On the other side are Christians who say truth, fulfillment, and perfection can only be found in Jesus. This is where the battle begins.

Could we parents be communicating the very messages we don't want our children receiving?

Getting Ready

Scriptures:
Matthew 19:21-26; 22:37-40; Hebrews 4:12, 13; Romans 3:9-18; 12:2; Exodus 20:1-3; Psalms 8:3-8; 119:1-4; John 15:26; Deuteronomy 26:16-19.

1. On newsprint, an overhead transparency, or the board, create a list of the eleven "-isms" as identified in Step 1. Do not include the cultural messages.
2. Photocopy "Cultural Messages" (RS-3A), and "Violent Acts" (RS-3B), making enough copies for everyone.

❶ What Is the World Saying to Us?

Objective:
To examine eleven common cultural messages that permeate our society and influence young and old alike (15 minutes).

Explain: **In this session, we will look at the messages our culture is giving us and focus on how they influence us as adults. Next session we will look at how they impact our children. As parents we are concerned about our children and the negative impact the secular culture has on them. But we are affected by the culture as well.**

Parents are the primary religious educators of their children, which is a serious responsibility. Therefore, periodically we need to examine our own thoughts and actions. Could we parents be communicating the very messages we don't want our children receiving?

There is discussion in religious education circles about the message of the faith becoming a curious mishmash of Biblical truth, cultural philosophies, and whatever we heard most recently on talk radio or Oprah. We don't want that to become true for us.

Display the list of eleven "-isms" written out ahead of time. Go over the "-isms" inviting the group members to define them and to identify the cultural messages of each one. (Use the suggested answers when needed.) Make sure the group basically agrees on the premise that these messages are permeating our culture. In many respects the messages flow together.

1. **Materialism:** The most important thing in life is the ownership of possessions.
2. **Existentialism:** Live for the moment; it's all that you have.
3. **Individualism:** The most important person in your life is you.
4. **Hedonism:** Pleasure, happiness, and fun are the primary purposes of life.
5. **Secularism:** God is not significant. At best He is irrelevant.

6. **Naturalism:** Human life has no more value than an owl or a tree.
7. **Utopianism:** Humans are basically good. Just give them a good environment and all evil will vanish.
8. **Anti-historicism:** Truth is relative and not as important as being politically correct.
9. **Pragmatism:** If it works do it.
10. **Moral relativism:** No absolutes. There are no rights, no wrongs.
11. **Victimism:** I am the way I am because of what other people have done to me.

Give every group member a copy of "Cultural Messages" (RS-3A), and allow the parents about five minutes to complete columns two and three individually. They will work on scriptural responses (column four) in the next step. Have them break into groups of five or less and discuss their responses in column 2 ("How is it [the message] being spread?") and column 3 ("How am I affected?"). Be ready to assist if needed according to the following information.

How Is It Being Spread?	Spiritual Responses
1. Media, peer pressure, athletic celebrities, advertising	May fulfill wants rather than needs, get-rich schemes
2. Literature, entertainment	Delay decisions with eternal significance
3. Schools, media, entertainment	Selfishness, take instead of give, prejudice
4. Arts, media, schools non-Christians	Pursuit of fun, lack of work ethic, entitlement, thrill-seeking
5. Government, literature, theater, schools	Ignore true God
6. "Rights" movements, schools, media	Abortion, euthanasia, casual regard for human life
7. Cults and "-isms," secular philosophies	No urgency to share the Good News

8. Media, entertainment	Leave the moorings of Scripture, rewrite history
9. Self-help movements, books, magazines, TV talk shows	Situational ethics
10. Secular philosophies and psychologies, media, justice system	Situational ethics, decisions based on emotions and not Scripture
11. Talk shows, justice system, schools, TV, entertainment	Sense of helplessness and hopelessness, avoidance of accountability, lack of responsibility

❷ What Does the Bible Say about These Messages?

Objective:
To examine the Scriptures and to begin the process of helping group members filter cultural messages through God's Word (15-25 minutes).

While the group members are still in their small groups, have them study the biblical passages referenced in the right-hand column of their work sheets, filling in what the Scripture has to say about the cultural messages. We are not trying to "proof-text" here, but rather point to the Scripture for advice and counsel. For some individuals this may be difficult. Some are better tuned to messages of the culture than to the Scriptures. Be prepared to help them out with suggestions:

1. Matthew 19:21-25—(Following Christ may cost us materially.)
2. Hebrews 4:12, 13—(We will have to give an account before God.)
3. Matthew 22:37-40—(Love your neighbor.)
4. Romans 12:2—(Don't allow the world to mold you.)
5. Exodus 20:1-3—(Have no other gods before God.)
6. Psalm 8:3-8—(We are valuable to God.)
7. Romans 3:9-18—(No one is perfectly good, we are all sinners.)
8. John 15:26—(The Holy Spirit will help us discern truth.)
9. Psalm 119:1-4—(Do things God's way.)
10. Deuteronomy 26:16-19—(Obey God's instructions.)
11. Matthew 19:26—(With God all things are possible.)

❸ "I'm Okay, You're Okay, Violence Is Okay"

Objective:
To see how violent acts can be justified by using cultural messages as the basis for immoral activities (10 minutes).

Pass out copies of "Violent Acts" (RS-3B) and have people pair up with someone other than their spouses. Assign each set of partners four or five "Violent Acts" statements to discuss, asking the question, **How might the person(s) involved justify his or her actions based on the cultural messages we've discussed?** Some people might disagree about whether or not some of the acts are necessarily violent. That's okay.

❹ How Can We Make Personal Changes?

Objective:
To suggest ways to change negative thinking and behaviors the group has discovered in this session in themselves and their families (5-10 minutes).

Up to this point, we have discussed the messages our culture is trying to make us listen to and obey and how they go against the counsel of God's Word. Let's brainstorm ways we can resist negative forces, individually and within our families. Make two columns on the board and list suggestions. Here are some ideas:

[Column 1] INDIVIDUALLY	[Column 2] FAMILY
Spend more time reading the Bible.	Implement family devotions.
Become aware of what your kids are looking at on TV and listen to some of their music. When you see philosophies being glorified that are not good, say so and explain why.	Spend more time talking to our kids about these influences and why they are not good. Give your children the opportunity to share their perspectives on these issues.
Be committed to make changes in your life when you see yourself following worldly philosophies.	Spend time doing activities with another family that is also trying to uphold similar principles.

Before closing in prayer, ask each individual to make a commitment to put at least one suggestion into practice this week in his or her personal life or in the family. Pray for the group and for their commitments.

Battling for the Minds of Our Kids!

4

Session Aim:
To help parents explore the impact of cultural messages on children and begin thinking about ways to counteract that impact.

Do you know people who believe everything that the culture tells them? If the world says, "eat, drink, and be trendy," they do it, without much thought. They work hard at "keeping up with the Joneses" and high stepping through society. The culture defines who they are and what they do. When I watch people like this, I'm amused.

However, if a violent dimension is added to these characteristics, tragedy can be the result.

I remember interacting with a family who bought into every negative cultural message imaginable. One of the sons, Del, went to summer camp with me. We arrived back in town at nine o'clock in the evening. I was awakened by Del's mother around four o'clock the next morning.

"Please come with me to the police station. They've arrested Del for murder. He didn't do it. He was at camp with you." As we drove to the police station Del's mother explained to me what happened. What she told me sent chills up my spine. "I'm glad Del was with you. I know he couldn't be involved. But, if he hadn't been with you, he might be the killer. He's like that, you know." Their whole family was living without a moral compass. Del had seemed like a nice kid at camp, but he was in a battle, and his heart, soul, and mind were severely wounded. The culture was winning. His own mother admitted it.

However, there is hope, for Del and others like him.

—*Mike Murphy*

It is important to note that not everything the culture says is evil.

Getting Ready

Scriptures:
Ephesians 6:10-18;
I John 2:15-17.

1. Make copies of "What Our Kids Are Saying Today" (RS-4A) and "The Whole Armor of God" (RS-4B) for everyone in the group.
2. Make copies of "Kids and the Media (RS-4C) to be handed out as preparation for Session 5. Make extra copies to have on hand next session for those who might forget to bring their copies to group. This resource is four pages.

❶ Kids Are Bombarded by Cultural Messages

Objective:
To examine the cultural messages that are being communicated to our children (10 minutes).

Last session we examined the impact of cultural messages on parents. In this session we want to look at the same messages, but this time in terms of how they affect our children.

It is important to note that not everything the culture says is evil. We want to avoid extreme culture-bashing or developing an "us" versus "them" attitude.

We are affected positively and negatively by our culture. We can enjoy great works of art, stirring music, and a variety of sports. We should be challenged as Christians when we discover secular institutions or figures expressing more compassion for the poor than do our churches or ourselves. It is important to acknowledge non-Christian performers and artists who have touched us in profound ways. God, of course, is the author of all that is beautiful. His hand is always at work, and we reap the benefit.

We will not explore all cultural aspects in depth nor give a balanced perspective on the entire culture. Our objective is to explain how cultural pressures or "-isms" —as we called them last time—contribute to an environment in which violence thrives.

Have the participants work independently on "What Our Kids Are Saying Today" (RS-4A). When they have finished, go over the comments, identifying the "-ism" represented by each one.

1. "If my old man was rich, then I could make it." (k. Victimism.)

2. "Yeah, I cheated. So what? I passed the test didn't I?" (i. Pragmatism.)

3. "I blew it this time, but give me time. I'll get better." (g. Utopian.)

4. "What's God ever done for me?" (e. Secularism.)

5. "Everybody else has the latest video recorder and we've got this old one." (a. Materialism.)

6. "What about me?" (c. Individualism.)

7. "When you die, that's it, right?" (f. Naturalism.)

8. "Just because it's wrong for you, doesn't mean it's wrong for me." (j. Moral relativism.)

9. "I'm going to enjoy myself as much as possible now. Tomorrow may never come." (b. Existentialism.)

10. "Party hearty! Have a good time." (d. Hedonism.)

11. "All politicians lie, so what?" (h. Anti-historicism.)

After going over the matching exercise, invite parents to share comments their own children might say. Then ask: **Is your son or daughter buying into these kind of messages? How could these messages be a building block toward violence in the lives of young people?** (Not every "-ism" has an obvious violent product, but here are some. *Materialism:* Hurting someone for something you want. *Individualism, hedonism, and secularism:* Combine to suggest that we do what gives us a thrill even if someone gets hurt. *Naturalism:* Abortion or euthanasia. *Pragmatism:* Doing whatever it takes [even murder or abuse] to get what you want. *Victimism:* Child or spouse abuse as modeled by parents. *Moral Relativism:* Do whatever you want, even take another person's life, if necessary.)

❷ Knowing the Battlefield

Objective:
To establish the spiritual dimension of the battle for children's minds and hearts (10 minutes).

Read the following statement by author Fran Sciacca:

There is a battle for the hearts and minds of teenagers today. I am convinced of it more than I've ever been before, that if we lose the battle for the minds of our young people, the entire understanding of the Judeo-Christian ethic which was so predominant from the foundation of this country to the present day, can be lost in one generation.[1]

We are in a spiritual battle with God on one side and Satan on the other.

Fran Sciacca makes a powerful statement. But we can win this battle and the Word of God tells us how.

Have everyone turn to Ephesians 6:10-18. Have volunteers read a verse or two.

What kind of battle is described here, and who are the opposing forces? (We are in a spiritual battle with God on one side and Satan on the other.)

What is necessary for victory in this kind of battle? (Dependence on God's strength and the whole armor of God.)

Distribute copies of "The Whole Armor of God" (RS-4B) and allow time for each person to answer the questions individually according to the instructions.

If some of the group members are not yet Christians, this is a good time to explain salvation based on faith in Christ and His provision for sin. If possible, talk individually with anyone who expresses an interest in becoming a Christian or wants more information about any of the pieces of "armor."

Have extra copies of the work sheet for parents to work through with their children at home. Encourage them to explain the spiritual defenses in terms the children can understand. This will help moms and dads see where their children's "armor" is weak so they will be able to pray more specifically with and for them.

❸ Creative Strategies for Battle

Objective:
To get group members to think creatively about conveying God's truth to their children (10-15 minutes).

What are some of the creative ways Satan relays his messages? (Movies, music, video, news coverage, talk shows, etc.) **Satan is a master at peddling illicit sex, illegal drugs, and violence. He has made it into a seductive art form, and his message appeals to kids. One way he works is to convince kids that their wants are really needs. How can we combat Satan's tactics and strategies?**

Have everyone turn to I John 2:15-17 while a volunteer reads the verses.

This persuasive passage gives the key to the Christian's battle strategy. It's encourages us to position ourselves on the high, strategic ground, where we will have the advantage over Satan. What is that strategic ground and how is it different from vulnerable ground? (The strategic ground has to do with goals, motives, and obedience to God's commands. When we crave the things of the world, we immediately become vulnerable to Satan's suggestions for how to acquire them and those methods often involve sin.) Note that the "world" is not trees and flowers, but all that stands antagonistic to God.

This passage also includes a promise for those who do the will of God. This can be a scriptural reference point as we try to help our kids deal with cultural messages. It is an encouraging portion of God's Word to meditate on and to share with our children. Where is our allegiance? To God or to the world? How is this allegiance evident in our daily lives?

Divide the group into four teams. Assign each team one of the sentences in I John 2:15-17.

> **Group 1:** "Do not love the world or anything in the world."
>
> **Group 2:** "If anyone loves the world, the love of the Father is not in him."
>
> **Group 3:** "For everything in the world—the cravings of sinful man, the lust of his eyes and the boasting of what he has and does—comes not from the Father but from the world."
>
> **Group 4:** "The world and its desires pass away, but the man who does the will of God lives forever."

Instruct the teams to rewrite their assigned section of the passage so it would make sense to a youth. Remind the teams to keep in mind the present battle for the hearts and minds of our kids. When they have completed their "modern translations," reconvene as one group, and put together the rewritten verses and read them. Here are possible answers:

"Do not love the world or anything in the world."— (Don't depend on the things this world offers for your happiness.)

"If anyone loves the world, the love of the Father is not in him." —(When you spend all of your time and effort trying to get ahead, acquire things, or make a name for yourself, it shows that you really do not love God.)

"For everything in the world—the cravings of sinful man, the lust of his eye, and the boasting of what he has and does—comes not from the Father but from the world." —(Desiring things that God says no to [like sex outside of marriage], wanting to buy everything you see, and thinking too highly of yourself because of money or a job are attitudes which do not come from God.)

"The world and its desires pass away, but the man who does

the will of God lives forever."— (Money, fame, power, all of these things will last a short time, but if you follow God's instructions, you will be most satisfied in this life and in heaven.)

---

❹ Ammunition for the Battle

Objective:
To begin the process of counteracting cultural messages being thrust upon our kids (10-15 minutes).

Our kids receive messages of all kinds from many sources, but what kind of messages do we want them to receive? (Follow Jesus. Be responsible. Avoid being influenced by the wrong crowd. Get good grades. Help the elderly and needy. Love and respect your parents. Work hard for things that last.)

Have you noticed how well the secular culture delivers its messages to people? Commercials are humorous. Movies are filled with action and suspense. Talk shows catch your attention with their "You may think you have heard everything, but listen to this" techniques.

How can parents and the church present truths from God's Word in a way that kids will take notice?

Allow the group to discuss this question. There isn't one correct answer, and it will be important to be respectful of any who question certain contemporary communication techniques. For instance, someone may think that Christian rock or rap music can be employed effectively. Another may think that we don't need to adopt the "world's methods" to communicate God's truth. However, if the group's conversation takes that turn, challenge the group members to offer something else that's better. Encourage them to provide examples of methods that have proved effective in today's culture.

Christians need to learn how to creatively communicate spiritual truth and grab the attention of our youth. This exercise is designed to help the parents communicate and think about creative responses to dangerous messages.

Divide the group into teams of three or four again. Give two sheets of paper to each team. Ask everyone to get out their copy of "What Our Kids Are Saying Today" (RS-4A) that they used in Step 1. Assign each team two or three of the cultural messages—depending on how many teams you have. Ask the teams to create alternative slogans, suitable for wearing on a T-shirt (by their sons or daughters), which counters the secular cultural messages. It should be a slogan a young person would feel comfortable wearing. It shouldn't be embar-

The young person today whose life represents the truth of God's Word stands out.

rassing, sound preachy, adult-like, or boring.

Have the teams share with the whole group the T-shirt slogans they have come up with. Then take a poll, voting on the best one. Have fun with this.

The purpose of this exercise is not to suggest that wearing T-shirts with slogans is the only or best way to communicate God's truths. Rather, it will encourage group members to think in ways that might communicate to today's kids. Several things can be gained from this exercise. Discuss the difficulty of coming up with something the kids might actually wear.

Ask: **Why was it so hard?** (Maybe we are not used to thinking creatively about how to package God's truth. God's truth is countercultural and slogans against God are easy to come up with.)

The young person today whose life represents the truth of God's Word stands out. To wear a T-shirt that boldly declares a Christian principle would require a commitment and the risk of ridicule. That is why we need to realize the seriousness of the battle we are in.

Ask: **What characterizes a battle?** (Battles are never easy, and there are casualties. To win the battle, one needs a strategy, and a plan). **Some of the best strategists and planners might be against Christ, but we should not despair. God knows how to plan too. In fact He is the master designer of all things. He is very imaginative and can give us many ingenious ideas to reach our youth for Christ. Maybe we should ask Him for His ideas.**

❺ Circle of Learning

Objective:
To have group members share about what they learned from today's session (5-10 minutes).

Have people stand in a circle. If you have a large group or are short on time, form two or three smaller circles. Go around each circle asking everyone to complete this sentence: "An insight I gained today is _____ ." (For instance, someone might say, "An insight I gained today is that I should not despise any means God uses to reach kids.")

Close in prayer in the same circle.

Preparation for Session 5: Pass out copies of "Kids and the Media" (RS-4C), asking the participants to read through it before the next session and to bring the resource sheet to group the next time. Warn your group members that they may be shocked by some of the facts presented in this material. Many parents may have no idea what kind of material the media is developing. Point out that the purpose of this resource is to help parents become more aware of what their kids are exposed to.

Close in prayer, asking God to give each person wisdom as he or she battles for the minds of today's kids.

Notes:

1. Fran Sciacca, *Generation At Risk: What Legacy Are the Baby Boomers Leaving Their Kids?* (Chicago: Moody Press, 1990, 1991), 22.

The Family and the Media

5

Session Aim:
To help parents examine their children's responses to the media and its messages and devise a plan for dealing with the negative aspects of the media.

What about it? Does the media promote violence or merely reflect what is already going on in society? Some people believe that if we could get rid of every song, television program, movie, or cartoon with a violent theme, then everything will be okay. It's true that the media is one of Satan's prime tools for destroying people's lives, but if we eliminated all negative cultural messages, Satan would find another avenue to spread his lies.

Nevertheless, while no one forces us to pay attention to the media, its all-pervasive nature means no one is immune from its influences. And the fact is, our young people are media-oriented. They hear and see things we never dreamed of when we were young. Unfortunately, they get a pretty unhealthy dose of violent images on a daily basis.

A steady diet of anything begins to take a toll. Listen and watch enough music, comedy routines, television, or films containing violent themes and pretty soon you either get bored with it all or consider yourself protected from its effects.

A steady diet of "violence" doesn't force people into a violence mode of operation, but it sure can lower their abhorrence of it and begin to distort their value systems.

What impact does the media have on your child and his or her friends? What can we do to help our children become more discerning in their media intake?

Children who have been extensively influenced by . . . the media might be called "culturally relevant, media-oriented children."

Getting Ready:

Scriptures:
II Timothy 3:1-5; Exodus 20:3, 4, 7, 8, 12-17; Matthew 4:10; 5:22, 28, 34; 12:36; Luke 12:15; 16:13.

1. You will need three sheets of newsprint or butcher paper and colored markers for each group for use in Step 1.
2. Cut a copy of "Hollywood vs. God's Commandments" (RS-5A) into strips and place them into a hat or some other container.
3. Make enough copies of "Media Helps for Our Home" (RS-5B) for everyone in the group.
4. Have extra copies of "Kids and the Media" (RS-4C) that you handed out last week for at-home reading.

❶ Our Children— the "Media-ites"

Objective:
To determine the characteristics of "culturally relevant, media-oriented children" and whether the parents' kids have any of those characteristics (10 minutes).

Divide the participants into three groups. Hand each group a large piece of newsprint or butcher paper. Everyone will have the same assignment.

Children who have been extensively influenced by the cultural messages displayed by the media might be called "culturally relevant, media-oriented children." Develop a list of a least five descriptive qualities of the "culturally relevant, media-oriented child." (Hints: knows a lot about the contemporary music scene, uses the right slang expressions, dresses exclusively according to the latest styles, spends most leisure time with the electronic media on, can mimic many media artists, has seen the latest movies, etc.)

After the groups have developed their lists of qualities, have them draw a creative picture of their "culturally relevant, media-oriented child" which portrays each of the five qualities listed. (Example: a head shaped like a television, ears that look like earphones, baggy trousers with money coming out of the pockets, the "right" foot gear, etc.) Have each group present its list of qualities and picture to the entire class.

Now, ask the group to imagine a continuum from "1" to "10" across the length of the room. On the continuum, "1" represents a child who is influenced very little by media, and "10" represents the child who is influenced greatly by media. Ask parents whether their children would be closer to a "1," a "10," or somewhere in between. Parents with more than one child can choose one child to represent. Have the parents notice responses of the other members of their small groups.

What do you think the position you chose on the continuum says about your children and how they are influenced by the media? (Have the parents discuss their responses in their small groups.)

All of us are influenced by media images and messages.

❷ At Least *I'm* Not Impacted by the Media

Objective:
To examine the media's ability to touch us all (5 minutes).

Reconvene the large group.

All of us are influenced by media images and messages. Why else would advertisers spend millions of dollars promoting their products if they couldn't influence buying habits? They even affect you. For instance, see how many of the following products or advertising slogans you know.

- **Michael Jordan and Charles Barkley are spokesmen for what brand of athletic shoes?** (Nike)
- **You deserve a break today at _____?** (McDonald's)
- **Dave Thomas is the media spokesman for what fast food chain?** (Wendy's)
- **During the Super Bowl, a beer company features a series of commercials showing beer bottles playing football. They call the game the ___ ____?** (Bud Bowl)
- **Please don't squeeze the _____?** (Charmin)
- **"You've got the right one, baby. Uh huh" is the theme for what brand of soft drink?** (Diet Pepsi) **Who sings the song?** (Ray Charles)
- **Rap group: Two Live _____?** (Crew)
- **Madonna's song: Like a _____?** (Virgin)
- **Movie: Menace II _____?** (Society)

The group will probably answer more than half of the questions fairly easily.

Recall of ad slogans does not necessarily mean that behavior will be affected. However, if advertising did not effectively influence many people, companies wouldn't spend the millions required to produce them. But more importantly, what many parents have known instinctively all along, has now been scientifically documented: "Seeing violence on television not only induces children to behave aggressively, it also plays a major role in making our society violence-prone. . . . In the last ten years some 20 long-term field studies have unanimously reached the same conclusion: There is a clear link between seeing violence on TV and behaving in an aggressive or violent manner. . . . Data from these studies and others suggest that if Americans did not watch television, the annual homicide rate would decrease by 10,000, the incidence of rape by 70,000, and the number of injurious assaults by 700,000."[1]

Hollywood's persistent hostility to religious values is not just peculiar, it is positively pathological.

What are some of the media's influences on your lives? (The media makes us more materialistic, more power hungry, more dissatisfied with life, etc.) Be sure to make the point that though we might be able to reduce the amount we listen to the media, it is virtually impossible to escape the barrage of the sights and sounds that come our way.

❸ Hollywood vs. God's Commandments

Objective:
To explore whether the media violates any of the Ten Commandments (10-15 minutes).

Some argue that the Ten Commandments are the basis of our laws and social rules of conduct. But we have veered from God's instructions. Presently, in our society, there is a loosely structured moral code in operation, but it doesn't all necessarily reflect God's moral code. The ungodly code glorifies violence, lack of honesty, disobedience, hatred, racial strife, sexual sins . . . the list goes on and on.

The media sends messages. Do those messages promote what Christians believe, or take a neutral or negative stand towards their belief system? Film critic Michael Medved believes Hollywood is hostile to religion and its values. Writing in *Hollywood vs. America*, he states:

> Hollywood's persistent hostility to religious values is not just peculiar, it is positively pathological. Rather than readjusting their view of reality in order to come to terms with the religious revival in America . . . most people in the movie capital simply choose to ignore what the surveys tell them. They retreat ever deeper into their precious and hermetically sealed little world of Malibu "enlightenment," and continue to write off all religious believers as so many slope-browed bumpkins who get their clothes from K-Mart and their ideas from the *National Enquirer*.[2]

This is a stinging indictment from a Hollywood, media insider who himself is not a Christian but Jewish. This is why Christians find the messages of the media so disturbing. We should be concerned about the negative impact on our children.

Ask six volunteers (who feel they are fairly media astute) to form two teams of three. Have them sit in chairs on either side of you facing the rest of the group. Announce a new game show called, "I've Seen It; I've Heard It; I've Played It."

Place the cut-up work sheet, "Hollywood vs. God's Command" (RS-5A), into a hat or some other container. As game show host, reach into the container and pick out one of the pieces of paper. Read it to the contestants.

For example, God says, **"You shall have no other gods before me,"** (Exodus 20:3)**, and "Worship the Lord your God, and serve him only,"** (Matthew 4:10)**.** Then ask the contestants: **Where have you seen or heard this message VIOLATED in today's media in the past six months?**

Anyone on either of the teams can yell out, "I've seen it," or "I've heard it," or "I've played it" and give an example.

The examples can come from any area of media—something visual (ads, movies, sitcoms, commercials, etc.), something audio (music, talk radio, etc.) or something played (video, party or board games, etc.). But the example must be specific. It can't be, "Oh, I hear stuff like that all the time."

Also, the examples must fit the phrase they call out. If they yell out "I've seen it," then the example must pertain to something they saw, not just listened to. The audience is the judge. If the audience agrees it is a good example, give that team a point. If the audience feels it isn't a good example, deduct a point. If a team provides a bad example, the other team can try to gain a point by supplying a more relevant one. The first team to earn five points wins.

Conclude the exercise by reading the following quote from Stephen Glenn, a youth ministry speaker. He writes about children and the media in his book, *Raising Self-Reliant Children in a Self-Indulgent World.*

For the first time in history, a generation of young Americans is receiving its impression about life passively from the media rather than from hands-on involvement with relevant activities. Generally, this perception of reality is deficient in teaching the skills of patience, personal initiative, hard work, and deferred gratification. On the contrary, results are achieved within a half hour by heroes who are pseudopsychopathic rebels, who achieve their objectives by breaking bones. On television, our youth see self-medication, drinking, casual sexuality, acts of violence, and miraculous solutions to problems. . . .

Essentially, there are five premises portrayed over and over. The first theme is that drinking or substance abuse is the primary activity in productive social relationships. . . . The second premise is that self-medication is the primary means of eradicating pain, discomfort, and boredom. . . . The third premise is that casual sexuality is the accepted norm. . . . The fourth premise conveyed by television is that acts of violence and lawlessness are acceptable solutions to problems. . . . The fifth premise is acted out primarily in commercials. It says that patience, deferred gratification, personal initiative, and hard work are unacceptable activities.[3]

❹ The Medium Is the Message

Objective:
To examine what the media is saying about today's kids (10-15 minutes).

Ask the parents to get out their copies of "Kids and the Media" (RS-4C). For those who did not get a copy last week or left it at home, provide extra copies. Ask for their reactions to the information. **Were they surprised? What did they learn? How did they feel as they read the material?**

Remind the participants that the subject of the media and children could be a whole course itself. Many adults do not understand the impact of sights and sounds on our lives. This handout is designed to give the group more insight.

As time allows, read one quote at a time. For quotes that are statements of opinion, ask the participants to stand if they agree or stay in their seats if they disagree. Allow the group to choose one or two quotes they would like to discuss further. If you are leading a large group, break into smaller ones.

Conclude this section with the following a quote from *Implications* magazine.

Studies show that parental involvement in the listening and viewing activities of/with their children alters the media's effects upon them as young people. We must find ways to encourage and help parents to enter the music worlds of their children.[4]

Emphasize that parents can make a difference in terms of the impact of the media has on their children. Limiting their children's exposure to the media may help some, but there are other creative responses too.

Media can be the conduit of all kinds of messages. The media is glamorizing many unholy activities.

❺ What Can We Do?

Objective:
To help parents develop a plan for dealing with media in their families (10-15 minutes).

Media can be the conduit of all kinds of messages. The media is glamorizing many unholy activities. Christian parents do not want their children thinking that rape, shooting, robbery, blasphemous speech, or any other from of violence is "cool!" But they often have very little idea of what to do.

Ask the group to suggest and discuss several drastic solutions parents might try in dealing with the media problem in their families. (Demanding the children never attend another movie; putting the television in the basement; destroying every CD in the house, etc.)

Why might these kinds of solutions be ineffective or have a backlash? (They could encourage rebellion. The children might resort to going to other people's homes to watch or listen to media—where the parents would have less control of the content. A blanket "No!" to media may take the emphasis off the importance of being discerning about the content and place it on the form of communication instead.)

What are some suggestions or guidelines for developing a media policy in your families? Ask the participants to suggest ideas that are scriptural, practical, and realistic. List their suggestions on the board. Indicate the age level to which each applies by using these symbols:

✔ = preschool   ✗ = grade school
★ = junior high or middle school   ? = high school

Pass out "Media Helps for Our Home" (RS-5B) for some additional ideas. If time permits, give the group an opportunity to fill out the last question on the bottom of the sheet.

Close in prayer, asking God for wisdom in selecting the most helpful responses for combating the negative influences of the media.

Notes:

1. David Neff, "Shootout at the Not-So-OK Corral," *Christianity Today,* Nov. 9, 1992, 12, 13. As summarized by InfoSearch.

2. Michael Medved, *Hollywood vs. America: Popular Culture and the War on Traditional Values* (San Francisco: Harper Collins and Grand Rapids, Mich.: Zondervan, 1992),72.

3. H. Stephen Glenn and Jane Nelsen, *Raising Self-Reliant Children in a Self-Indulgent World* (Rocklin, Calif.: Prima Publishing and Communications, 1989), 42.

4. Center for Youth Studies, Gordon Conwell Theological Seminary/ Young Life *Implications* magazine, Summer 1989, 9.

My Baby a Troublemaker? No!

6

Session Aim:

To define normal behaviors and examine the qualities needed in a child's life to help him or her deal effectively with a violent culture.

Please help me! Last week, Allen, my fifteen-year-old nephew got into an argument with a seventeen-year-old neighborhood boy. The older boy cursed at my nephew and pushed him around. The boys who watched told the story like this.

After Greg pushed Allen, Allen stood there for a minute, as though he was going to fight back. Then Allen just took off running. We thought he was just mad and went home to blow off some steam. We went on playing ball. About ten minutes later, Allen came back, pulled out a pistol and shot Greg. Popped him, just like that!

Before this tragedy, Allen seemed okay, just a typical teenager. At the last family gathering he laughed along with us as we reminisced about our crazy teenage years. Sure, my sister occasionally had to talk to Allen's teachers when he fell behind in his school work, and he had gotten into a fist fight or two. But those seemed like ordinary, growing up problems. We never imagined he would do something like this.

As I write this, I can hear my own two boys in the next room arguing over whose turn it is as they play Nintendo. I'm concerned about them. Is there something specific I should watch for? How can I prevent this tragedy from happening to them? I'm afraid, very afraid!

—*A worried mother*

Determinedly going against everything one's parents say may represent a deeper rebellion.

Getting Ready

Scriptures:
Acts 20:7-12; Luke 2:41-52.

1. Make a copy of "Who Am I?" (RS-6A), "External Assets" (RS-6B), and "Internal Assets" (RS-6C) for everyone.

❶ I Drove My Parents Crazy

Objective:
To determine whether the behaviors group members engaged in as teenagers were normal or abnormal (10-15 minutes).

When you were young, what behaviors did you or your friends do that drove your mother or father crazy? Allow time for parents to respond. Down the left side of your board or newsprint, list those behaviors. (They might include things like staying out late without calling, talking back to parents, fighting with a sibling, smoking, experimenting with drinking, listening to rock 'n' roll music, driving too fast.)

Which of these behaviors do you now think were normal for teenagers back then? Put a plus sign next to all those activities that were normal and a minus sign next to the ones the group considers abnormal. Encourage the group to discuss why some things were normal while others were abnormal. For instance, some experimentation is normal. But determinedly going against everything one's parents say may represent a deeper rebellion. Or, while it is common for young people to think that they are so invulnerable that they go without a coat in cold weather or jump off a garage roof, excessively reckless behavior may indicate a lack of self-esteem, a sense of futility in life, or even a death wish.

Down the right side of the board, list the behaviors the group members' children are involved in that drive them crazy. **What areas are similar or different?** Keep both lists on the board for use again in Step 3.

❷ Even Kids in the Bible Did Some Amazing Stuff

Objectives:
To evaluate behaviors of today's kids in light of some scriptural insights about growing up (10 minutes).

Sometimes when reading the Bible, we put on a "holy" face and get very serious in our examination of the passage as we try to be profound. But as we study the following two passages, put on your "humorous" face and attempt to look at them in a different way.

Acts 20:7-12 and Luke 2:41-52

Ask for a volunteer to read Acts 20:7-12.
How did Eutychus [EU-tih-cuss] behave? (He fell asleep in church.) **How is this typical of a young person?** (It expresses boredom, inattentiveness to spiritual things,

doing inappropriate things at the wrong time.) **If you had been across the room watching your son fall asleep while Paul was talking, what would have been your reaction?** Allow the participants to offer their own reactions. **We will come back to this passage but let's look at the next one first.**

Now ask for a volunteer to read Luke 2:41-52.

How old was Jesus in this familiar story of His talking with the elders in the temple? (Twelve.)

Put yourself in Mary and Joseph's place. What would you be thinking and feeling when you noticed Jesus missing? (Embarrassed, scared, frustrated.)

After Jesus was found, what would be your thinking and feelings? (Relieved, angry, confused.)

How had Jesus acted like an early adolescent? (Adventurous, He was off on His own while His parents worried.)

Both of these passages are fun, when you observe them from a developmental point of view. Eutychus was at an evening service that had extended long into the evening. The room was crowded and probably hot. He was bored and fell asleep. If we were watching him nod off, we'd probably be upset at his lack of respect. On the other hand, we might envy his youthful freedom. God loved Eutychus. He had him brought back to life.

Jesus was twelve when the incident at the temple occurred. Here was a twelve year old and His parents were worrying. The passage says that Jesus grew. Maybe this preteen adventure was one of the learning experiences in His life. It certainly was for Mary and Joseph.

❸ My Hormones Made Me Do It

Objective:
To explore the normal side of growing up (10 minutes).

Read the following quote from James Dobson's book, *Parenting Isn't for Cowards*. It talks about two issues confronting young adolescents.

The first and most important [change] is hormonal in nature. I believe parents and even behavioral scientists have underestimated the impact of the biochemical changes occurring in puberty. . . . The emotional characteristics of a suddenly rebellious teenager are rather like the symptoms of . . . a tumultuous mid-life crisis. . . . Understanding this

glandular upheaval makes it easier to tolerate and cope with the emotional reverberations that are occurring. For several years, some kids are not entirely rational!

The other is social in nature. It is common knowledge that a twelve- or thirteen-year-old child suddenly awakens to a brand new world around him, as though his eyes were opening for the first time. That world is populated by age mates who scare him out of his wits. His greatest anxiety, far exceeding the fear of death, is the possibility of rejection or humiliation in the eyes of his peers.[1]

Go back to the behaviors listed on the board. Ask the group to identify whether those behaviors were or are motivated by hormonal or social factors or both.

❹ What Keeps Normal from Becoming Horrible?

Objective:
To help parents recognize the difference between normal behavior and at-risk behavior in their children (15-25 minutes).

Jane Nelsen and Lynn Lott in their book, *I'm On Your Side*, call the process of growing up through adolescence "individuation." That's a fancy word for trying to figure out who you are and what you're supposed to be doing by establishing yourself as other than an extension of your parents. But the process is often unsettling to the family and parents frequently wonder, "Does it have to be like this?"

Pass out the work sheet "Who Am I?" (RS-6A). Since they wrote the statements on this work sheet, Jane Nelsen and Lynn Lott obviously agree with them, but you might have your doubts. Have everyone read through them and indicate on the agree/disagree scales how they respond to the statements. When the group members have finished the exercise, ask for discussion on any points where some parents disagreed. Don't try to force agreement, but let the experience of some parents impact the opinions of others.

Explain that everyone goes through developmental stages in life. Adolescence is a term that once described the time between the ages of twelve and eighteen. Now, adolescence could start at nine or ten and extend into the late twenties or early thirties. There are physical and social reasons for this. Physically, young people are reaching puberty much earlier than in the past. But socially they are not equipped to compete in the adult world until much later.

Don't assume youth know how much you love them.

Let's be realistic about life. This is a crazy world. The normal individuation process, with all its hormonal and social pressures, can become abnormal pretty easily. Are there things to help kids stay on the normal side of behavior and grow up healthy?

The Search Institute of Minneapolis has conducted research around "assets" that promote positive teenage development. These assets may result from "external" factors such as positive relationships in family, friendship groups, school, community, or church. Or they may result from "internal" factors reflecting the teenager's personal convictions, values, and attitudes.

Distribute copies of "External Assets" (RS-6B) and "Internal Assets" (RS-6C). Then divide the group into an even number of teams with no more than three members per team. Ask half of the teams to work on coming up with suggestions for how they as parents can enhance the external assets for their children while the other teams come up with suggestions for enhancing internal assets.

When they have finished, have those who worked on the external assets share their ideas with those who worked on the internal assets and vice versa. If you have the time, you can do this sharing as a large group so that more creative ideas are shared. If your time is limited, have smaller teams share with each other.

It will be most useful if the parents come up with their own ideas. However, the following are some ideas suggested by Search Institute for each asset. Be prepared to share ideas as appropriate.

External Assets (RS-6B)[2]

1. Family support—(Give more hugs and verbal encouragement; don't assume youth know how much you love them. Set aside at least one evening per week for family activities.)

2. Parents as social resources—(Ask youth every day about what they are doing and thinking about. Give youth space when they need it, but let them know you're always available—and then be available.)

3. Parent communication—(Regularly ask youth questions about what they think and believe. Have topical family dinners every once in a while in which the whole conversation focuses on one topic.)

4. Other adult resources—(Give your children opportunities to spend time with other adults. Plan vacations with other families your children enjoy—especially the parents.)

5. Other adult communication—(Encourage your teens to call an adult friend whom they respect when they need advice. Include youth in conversations in the home with other adults.)

6. Parent involvement in school—(Make it a point to talk with all of your child's teachers during the school year. Regularly ask your teens what they are learning in school. Offer to help with homework in appropriate ways.)

7. Positive school climate—(Report any concerns you have about your child feeling uncomfortable or unsafe in school. Volunteer in the school to tutor and support students.)

8. Parental standards—(Regularly renegotiate family rules with teenagers so they are developmentally appropriate and consistently and fairly enforced. Talk with other parents when you're not sure how to respond to a particular situation.)

9. Parental discipline—(Be consistent in rules enforcement. Do not let discipline become an excuse for violently venting anger at your teenager.)

10. Parental monitoring—(Have a family calendar where everyone notes personal activities. Always ask who teens will be with when they go to parties or other activities.)

11. Time at home—(Set limits on how often youth can go out with friends during the school week. Do not let a teenager work more than fifteen hours during the school week.)

12. Positive peer influence—(Invite your children's friends to spend time in your home. Get to know them. Talk with your teens about their friends. Ask probing questions. Affirm positive friendships.)

13. Music—(Don't complain when your child plays drums all afternoon. As much as possible, provide opportunities for musical involvement by providing an instrument, lessons, and time to practice.)

14. Extracurricular activities—(Sponsor or coach a club in a subject area of personal interest. Talk with your teens about matching personal interests with extracurricular opportunities.)

15. Community activities—(Car pool with other families so that youth can participate in community activities. Support community organizations as a volunteer or through financial contributions.)

16. Church involvement—(Allow teens to be part of decisions about where to attend worship services. Encourage active involvement in religious activities by modeling active involvement.)

Internal Assets (RS-6C)[3]

1. Achievement motivation—(Model an ongoing interest in learning and new discoveries. Seek to understand and address the fears and motivations that may lie behind any apathy or resistance toward school.)

2. Educational aspiration—(Talk with your teenager about life goals, priorities, and dreams. Commit to helping support your teen through post-high school education.)

3. School performance—(Affirm school success through family celebrations. Stay in contact with teachers about progress; don't wait for a report card.)

4. Homework—(Provide a comfortable place for your teen to study without distractions. Turn off the television and limit hours on after-school jobs. Be sensitive to individual learning styles. Some kids need controlled background music, some need bright lights, some need low lights, etc.)

5. Values helping people—(Regularly spend family time helping others—and talking about why you do it. Encourage and support your teen to take [reasonable] personal risks to help other people.)

6. Global concern—(Include your teen in family discussion about how to contribute to charitable organizations. Take family vacations in which you expose your teenager first-hand to a world issue.)

7. Empathy—(Model mutual respect in the family. Do not tolerate put-downs. Listen to your teenager express his or her feelings, and teach him or her to listen to others.)

8. Values sexual restraint—(Make your family's expectations clear. Teach and model appropriate ways to show affection.)

9. Assertiveness skills—(Listen to your teen's beliefs, and help him or her learn to articulate those beliefs. Model appropriate assertiveness in standing up for what you believe.)

10. Decision-making skills—(Include your teen in family decisions—and explain the decision-making process. Don't blow up over a poor decision; help your teen learn from it.)

11. Friendship-making skills—(Give teenagers ideas of creative things they can do with friends. Emphasize friendships in your own life and encourage your teen to invite friends to your home.)

12. Planning skills—(Have family meetings to talk about future plans; discuss priorities and reasoning. Give your teen responsibility for some planning for the family.)

13. Self-esteem—(Regularly express your love—verbally and nonverbally—to your teenager. Respect and celebrate your teen's uniqueness.)

14. Hope—(Inspire hope by being hopeful. Don't dismiss a teen's dreams as naive.)

When the exchange of ideas has been completed, reassemble the whole group. Have parents take a few moments to reflect on where their kids are. Ask them to place a star in front of the three strongest assets for their children. Than have them circle three suggestions on each of their resource sheets that they could work on to increase their children's assets.

Then close in prayer. If your group is comfortable with praying aloud together, have volunteers finish these prayer statements:

Lord, thank You for _____ .
Lord, please help me _____ .

Notes:

1. James Dobson, *Parenting Isn't for Cowards* (Waco, Tex.: Word Books, 1987), 144-146.
2. "Ideas for Building External Assets in Youth," *Youth Update*, August 1993, 4, 5. Used by permission of Search Institute.
3. Ibid.

What Puts Joey (or Jane) "At Risk?"

7

In this session you will be introduced to a boy named Joey (or it could be a girl named Jane). Joey is "at risk." This means he is often in some kind of trouble.

At-risk kids like Joey are not a new phenomenon. Huck Finn was a troublemaker. Remember Fat Albert and the Cosby kids? How about the Li'l Rascals and Fonzie from "Happy Days?" Hollywood writers and novelists have turned at-risk behavior into some of the most entertaining scenarios.

You will find at-risk kids in the Bible, also. The activities of the prodigal son probably raised a few eyebrows in his neighborhood. And did you ever wonder why James and John were called "Sons of Thunder?" Were they perhaps troublemakers?

However, the at-risk Joeys and Janes we meet today are not interesting biblical characters or amusing television stars. They are juvenile delinquents, troublemakers, misfits, gang-bangers, and skinheads. They live in posh suburban areas, farming communities, and low-income urban centers. Unfortunately, their activities are not daring adventures or harmless pranks. Most at-risk youngsters are in deep trouble, making big mistakes, and scarring themselves for life.

Usually, an at-risk Joey or Jane is easy to spot, unless he or she happens to be living in your home. Sentiment can sometimes cause a parent to put blinders on and make excuses for some pretty uncivilized behavior.

*S*entiment can sometimes cause a parent to put blinders on and make excuses for some pretty uncivilized behavior.

Getting Ready

Scriptures:
II Samuel 13:1, 8-14, 21-29, 37-39; 14:21-33; 15:1-10, 13, 14; 18:9-15, 33.

1. Photocopy enough copies for everyone of "Signs of Trouble! There's a Storm Brewing" (RS-7A).
2. Calculate how many teams of no more than four people each your group would make. Then make as many copies of "The Life of Absalom" (RS-7B) as you will have teams. (Make a few extra copies in case participants want intact copies later.) Cut apart a sheet for each team as indicated and place the strips plus the top of the resource sheet in an envelope, and number the envelope. Each team will get an envelope with a complete cut-apart sheet in it.
3. Prepare enough copies of "Could My Child Turn Out Like Joey?" (RS-7C) so that parents may complete one for each child.

❶ Meet At-Risk Joey

Objective:
To help parents discover indicators of at-risk behavior (10-20 minutes).

Hand out the work sheet "Signs of Trouble! There's a Storm Brewing" (RS-7A). Ask participants to read through the list of behaviors that a variety of experts have determined may be indicators of potential problems. Then read—or have a volunteer read—the following case study of Joey. When you are finished, have participants check off on their work sheets the at-risk behaviors Joey is exhibiting.

> **Joey is fourteen years old. He lives in a suburb directly adjacent to a very large city. Like many communities, it is diverse economically, ethnically, and racially.**
>
> **He should be a freshman in high school but was held back in fifth grade so he could work on basic skills. Even though he is very bright, teachers are concerned that he doesn't take school very seriously. He only uses a limited portion of his potential. Joey shrugs his shoulders and says, "I don't care," when he is questioned about his school performance. He's been absent quite a bit lately.**
>
> **Joey was an all-star Little League player in seventh grade, but has decided not to play in eighth grade or high school. Joey says, "All the coaches I know are stupid. They never let people play the game the right way."**
>
> **Joey and his parents attended church regularly at one time, but Joey's dad got into an argument**

Most at-risk youngsters are in deep trouble, making big mistakes, and scarring themselves for life.

with the minister, and they quit attending. They don't even go to church on Easter or Christmas anymore.

Joey has a girlfriend. He used to have conservative morals but is now thinking of how he can get his girlfriend to have sex with him.

Joey's friends used to be the kids in his immediate neighborhood. But in the past year, he began to hang out with some older kids, several blocks away. Whenever he is with his new friends, he wears a certain kind of clothes and certain colors. When Joey's new friends call, they don't ask for him by name; they ask for "Boogie." Joey says, "Don't worry, it's just a nickname. It doesn't mean anything."

Joey spends his evenings with those friends. On weekends, he rarely comes home. His mother and father say, "We just can't control his coming and going anymore."

Last semester, Joey's parents were called to the high school. The principal said Joey was running with the wrong crowd, a crowd that was involved in some illegal activity. He didn't have any proof of wrongdoing by Joey, but wanted to alert the parents. Joey's father got into a shouting match with the principal. He was angry because the principal made them come down to the school and made them look bad, all "for nothing." "After all," Joey's father said, "I don't need the school telling me how to raise my kid."

That night Joey's father warned him to stay away from his "goofball friends." Joey argued back and his father began yelling and slapping Joey around until Joey just stomped out of the house, slamming the door behind him.

The music Joey listens to has a very rebellious tone. His mother read in the newspaper that his favorite group advocated beating up your girlfriend and raping her if you wanted to. When she asked Joey about it, he said, "I don't even pay any attention to what they are saying. I just like listening to the beat and dancing to it."

Most importantly, these kids need the hope that comes from new life in Christ.

Joey doesn't work, but he and his buddies always seem to have plenty of money. He smokes cigarettes regularly now and sometimes his mother thinks she smells the smoke of marijuana on his clothes.

After you have allowed the participants time to check off indicators of potential problems on their work sheets, ask the following questions. **What is Joey at-risk for, or in other words, what could his behavior be leading to?** (Joey is at-risk for dropping out of school, fathering a child out of wedlock, gang activity, unlawful activities, drug dependency, violence, etc.) **What behaviors may be indicative of approaching violence?** (Father is violent with him. Drugs and gang activity may be involved. Joey is not bothered by lyrics advocating violence.)

If you are leading an hour-long session, divide the group into several teams. (Otherwise, go on to Step 2.) Ask teams to come up with ideas that might make a difference in Joey's life. Acknowledge that at-risk kids often need help of many kinds. Most importantly, these kids need the hope that comes from new life in Christ

❷ Observing an At-Risk Joey in the Bible

Objective:
To help parents understand the danger of ignoring at-risk indicators (10 minutes).

Have the participants divide up into teams of about four people each. Give each team an envelope containing the cut-apart resource sheet, "The Life of Absalom" (RS-7B), according to the instructions in the Getting Ready section of this session. Conduct a contest to see which team can most quickly unscramble Absalom's life by arranging the strips in chronological order. Remind the teams that if they are unfamiliar with this Bible story, they may use the Bible passages listed on the top of the resource sheet.

The following is the correct order:

1. Absalom's sister Tamar is raped by their stepbrother Amnon, one of David's son's (II Sam. 13:1; 8-14).

2. David heard about the rape, and he was angry, but did nothing about it (II Sam. 13:21).

3. Absalom said nothing to Amnon after the rape of his sister, but two years later he had Amnon killed to avenge him for raping his sister (II Sam. 13:22-29).

4. Absalom fled after killing Amnon, and went to Geshur (where his mother's father and relatives lived), and David mourned for his son daily, but did nothing (II Sam. 13:37-39).

5. David sent for Absalom to return from Geshur to Jerusalem, but David took a long time to forgive Absalom and didn't want to see him. Absalom lived in Jerusalem for two years before David allowed him to come see him (II Sam. 14:21-33).

6. After seeing David, Absalom still rebelled and got several men to follow him. He revolted against his father and ran David out of the city and made himself king (II Sam. 15:1-10; 13, 14).

7. David's men pursued Absalom to restore David to the throne. They found Absalom hanging from a tree. He was then killed as he hung from the tree (II Sam. 18:9-15).

8. David wept bitterly and mourned the death of his son (II Sam. 18:33).

After you finish unscrambling the story, discuss the following questions:

Why would Absalom be considered an at-risk child? (He was violent, rebellious, angry, revengeful, and undisciplined; he did not have a good home life; etc.)

How did his father contribute to his negative behavior? (He would not forgive him, would not communicate with him, and was not attentive to his son's concerns and needs.)

Why is it unwise for parents to ignore negative behavior? (Overlooking at-risk behavior could lead to worse behavior or deadly consequences, fragment the family, cause everyone to suffer and other severe problems.)

What are some elements that could have been introduced into Absalom's life that might have kept him from such a tragic end? (His father could have taken time to help Absalom understand spiritual truths. Someone else could have been there for Absalom to talk to when David wasn't available. He could have turned to God for forgiveness and help.)

*J*oey has no relationship with Jesus Christ. . . . lacks some basic skills and perceptions. . . . has a home life that is up for grabs.

❸ Could My Child Turn Out Like Joey?

Objective:
To allow parents to evaluate their own children in light of at-risk behaviors (10 minutes).

Ask participants to fill out the resource sheet "Could My Child Turn Out Like Joey?" (RS-7C) for each of their children, then answer the questions at the bottom. Encourage parents to be very honest in their evaluation.

❹ Let's Help Joey

Objective:
To identify factors that might give Joey a second chance (15-20 minutes).

Assure the group that the possible scenario about Joey's future does not have to come true. If other factors are introduced into Joey's life at this point, Joey may be able to beat the odds. Remember to give participants encouragement throughout this process. Hopefully, very few people in your group will have a "Joey or Jane" in their home. However, some participants may be seeing enough negative indicators in their children's lives to seriously worry them.

What causes children to turn out like Joey? Perhaps if we can understand some of the factors that contribute to at-risk behavior, we can take steps to deal with them. There are no easy answers. Kids from great families develop at-risk tendencies while other kids from horrible homes seem to do well. Sometimes kids from stable homes commit violent acts at the same time kids who aren't sure who Dad is and are being raised by an incompetent mother, end up going to Harvard and making positive contributions. The home situation is a major factor, but not the only ingredient.

However, while there are no formulas or magic keys, there is growing evidence of the causes of at-risk behavior. Here are three reasons why Joey is at-risk:

1. **Joey has no a relationship with Jesus Christ.**
2. **Joey lacks some basic skills and perceptions about himself that are needed to make him an effective person.**
3. **Joey's home life is up for grabs.**

Explain that the next activity is to "help" Joey and his parents. He has been arrested for petty theft. Instruct the group to imagine that they have been invited to offer some

53

help to Joey and his family in the form of letters. Form four teams and give these assignments:

Team 1: Write Joey about becoming a Christian.
Team 2: Write and help Joey change his negative perception about himself and his circumstances.
Team 3: Encourage Joey about his home life and offer alternatives to help.
Team 4: Write a letter to Joey's parents suggesting ways that they might help Joey.

Encourage each group to use at least one Scripture passage in the letter. They should keep in mind that Joey is only fourteen. The letters should be short, to the point, and not preachy to him. (Possible Scriptures: Team 1—John 1:12; Team 2—I Cor. 10:13; Team 3—Ps. 103; Team 4—Prov. 22:6.)

After five or ten minutes, have the group reconvene and share their letters.

After Team 1 reads its letter encouraging Joey to become a Christian, share the following comment by Gordon McLean, a Christian youth worker, particularly experienced in working with gang members.

> **I spoke at a Chicago conference sponsored by law enforcement and neighborhood groups offering ways to deal with the gangs and was introduced by the words, "Now we will have Mr. McLean discuss the religious option." That really got to me, so I grabbed the microphone and said, "We are not just another option; we are all there is!" What I meant was that unless God did a miracle in a kid's life, remaking him from the inside out, then every other community effort to solve the problems of youth violence was found to fail. Education, family counseling, recreation, law enforcement, job training— all are good and important in their place but never a substitute for spiritual rebirth.[1]**

After Team 2 shares its letter encouraging Joey's self perception and outlook on life, read the following.

> **In his book,** *Raising Self-Reliant Children in a Self-Indulgent World,* **Stephen Glenn says that for at-risk young people to become low-risk individuals they need to develop** *strong . . .*

1. Perceptions of personal capabilities: "I am capable."
2. Perceptions of significance in primary relationships: "I contribute in meaningful ways and I am genuinely needed."
3. Perceptions of personal power or influence over life: "I can influence what happens to me."
4. Intrapersonal skills: The ability to understand personal emotions, use that understanding to develop self-discipline and self-control, and learn from experience.
5. Interpersonal skills: The ability to work with others and develop friendships through communication, cooperation, negotiation, sharing, empathizing, and listening.
6. Systematic skills: The ability to respond to the limits and consequences of everyday life with responsibility, adaptability, flexibility, and integrity.
7. Judgment skills: The ability to use wisdom and evaluate situations according to appropriate values.[2]

After Teams 3 and 4 read their letters about Joey's home life, make this comment: **When "home" is a rocky place, it's hard on children. Kids who have good, strong homes where they feel safe and secure, deal with a violent, upside-down world more effectively than children who don't. It's never too late to start smoothing out the bumps in a rocky home life. No matter how bad it looks, you can take a step in another direction. It's the only step worth taking.**

Before closing in prayer ask the participants to think of one plan of action they can put into practice this week to nurture or strengthen their children. Challenge them to pray specifically for that area.

Close by having couples pray with each other. If there are single parents, have them form pairs or triads.

Notes:

1. Gordon McLean with Dave and Neta Jackson, *Cities of Lonesome Fear* (Chicago: Moody Press, 1993), 75.

2. H. Stephen Glenn and Jane Nelsen, *Raising Self-Reliant Children in a Self-Indulgent World* (Rocklin, Calif: Prima Publishing and Communications, 1989), 49, 50.

The First Defense: A 8 Strong Family

Session Aim:
To help parents understand how to build a strong family unit which can combat violence.

Family . . . what a wonderful concept! God created, established, and delights in it. Remember the original family? Adam and Eve ran into a few problems when Satan launched his first attack on the family in the garden of Eden. They suffered through a terrible violent confrontation between their two sons, Cain and Abel. One son was unfairly murdered, and the other son was the cold-blooded killer. But God did not give up. He continued to nurture His original family plan.

Unfortunately we have veered from what God had in mind. The family is often deemed unimportant. Too few people commit themselves to work at family development. Some people with a non-biblical perspective want to reshape the family into something God never intended.

The family was designed to be a major building block for children. God desired for the family to be a place where values are transmitted, dreams are nurtured, and faith is caught.

How do you raise kids in a violent culture? Help your family become as strong as possible—a place where love abounds between parents and children.

In the next three sessions, we will be looking at the family. What makes it strong? How can parents develop habits of effective parenting? How can we get rid of behaviors that hinder us from being the family God wants us to be?

*F*amily . . . *what a wonderful concept! God created, established, and delights in it.*

Getting Ready

Scriptures:
Luke 15:11-32.

1. Have the following questions written on a board or newsprint when the class begins. Cover the questions with something until you are ready to use them.
   - How is the family in the Scripture like a family today?
   - How is the family in the Scripture different from a family today?
   - Why do you think Jesus used the family unit as the setting for this teaching?
   - What were the strengths of this family?
   - What were its weaknesses?
   - What do you think Jesus is trying to teach us about God's family?
2. Put up six paper banners around the room. Each banner should have a separate heading and plenty of room to write below it. The banner headings should be as follows:
   - Commitment to the Family
   - Spend Time Together
   - Have Good Family Communication
   - Express Appreciation to Each Other
   - Have a Spiritual Commitment
   - Able to Solve Problems in a Crisis
3. Photocopy "Solutions for the Picky Shopper" (RS-8A), "The Prodigal Son Improv" (RS-8B) and "Looking at the Strength of Our Family" (RS-8C) for each group member.

❶ Family? In Today's Culture? Who Are You Kidding?

Objective:
To reinforce the essential nature of family in the current day (10 minutes).

What do we need to do to help our kids? Build a new recreational center? Try to find better counselors? Improve the school system? Spend more money? Offer job training? That's the ticket!

No, it's not.

Tony Evans, a widely respected pastor, described the following situation in *Urban Family* magazine:

> **One day a mother and father took their child to a toy store to buy him something to play with. A store clerk walked endlessly up and down each aisle as the kid rejected every toy the clerk showed him. The parents became increasingly frustrated with the clerk's inability to find something suitable for their child's entertainment and pleasure.**
>
> **Exasperated, they defiantly looked at the clerk**

Children are dying because adults have lost sight of their fundamental duty: To protect and nurture our future. . . .

and asked, "Why can't you find our child an acceptable toy!" Equally frustrated, the clerk responded, "Folks, what this kid needs we don't sell here. He needs _____ !"[1]

The answer is "parents." But do not reveal it at this point. Instead, distribute copies of "Solutions for the Picky Shopper" (RS-8A) and have the group members select which answers they think would be most helpful to this boy.

When the groups have finished, ask them which ideas they eliminated, and then allow them to compare the order of the remaining ideas. Be sure to take note of any ideas not on the list that the group members contributed. When everyone has responded, reveal that the answer Tony Evans intended was "parents." Explain that he was trying to show how easy it is to try to fill voids with all kinds of things, but they don't work.

Why is family so important? An article from the *Chicago Tribune* entitled, "Sixty-One Young Victims Leave Behind a Trail of Anger, Abuse, and Blame," reports:

> There were sixty-one children killed in the Chicago area [in 1993]. They were shot, beaten, shaken, stabbed or starved. They were killed on the streets and in their homes. They were killed by their parents, by their neighbors, by friends and by strangers. . . . The victims seldom have a functional family to protect them.
>
> Children are dying . . . they are born to parents who have so little understanding of how to raise a child that they respond to a baby's crying with their fists. . . . Children are dying because adults have lost sight of their fundamental duty: To protect and nurture our future. . . . Above all else, children are dying because their families are failing them. An overriding lesson to be drawn from a year of grim storytelling is this: American families are fractured, and little else can be fixed until we begin to fix them.[2]

Ask: **Why do so many people appear so unwilling to accept the fact that disintegrating family life is at the core of many of our culture's problems?** Talk about this issue. Write ideas on the board. Emphasize the point that the

God ordained the family to be the primary building block of the culture.

family structure has a powerful impact on our children. Perhaps personal responsibility is at the core of the problem. People would much rather blame something they can't control than take responsibility for what they can.

Conclude this step by saying: **God ordained the family to be the primary building block of the culture. This institution needs to be strong and vital. If our kids are going to have a fighting chance to grow up healthy and whole in a violent culture, families are going to have to be strong. That's a message that many people don't want to hear.**

❷ The Family . . . God Knows What He's Doing

Objective:
To examine the story of the prodigal son to emphasize God's high view of the family (10-25 minutes).

If your session is only forty-five minutes long, have someone read Luke 15:11-32 and move on to discuss the questions. Otherwise do "The Prodigal Son Improv."

Pass out copies of "The Prodigal Son Improv" (RS-8B) and divide your group into four dramatic teams. Assign each team to portray one of the scenes in a different dramatic style. Let the groups go over their scene descriptions briefly and select the style of their choice provided no other team has chosen the same style. That is, first-come-first-served on the style selections. Then give the teams about five minutes to plan how they are going to act out their scenes. It will be primarily an improvisation, so no rehearsal and only limited planning should be needed. Tell the teams that they have only three minutes to portray their scene. You will have to keep this whole step moving rapidly.

Encourage everyone to have a lot of fun with this and to ham it up! Encourage use of exaggerated accents and actions within their styles. Group members should consult Luke 15:11-32 for additional details to the story.

After the improv or the reading of the passage, discuss the following questions.

How is the family in these Scriptures like a family today? (Rebellious children, faithful children, jealousy in the families, living like partying and having a good time are the most important things in the world.)

How is the family unlike some families today? (Forgiving, peacemaking family, father has a predominant role, and demonstrates wise actions.)

Why do you think Jesus uses the family unit as the

*ffective family life does not just happen;
it is the result of deliberate intention,
determination and practice.*

primary setting for this important teaching? (The family is important to Him; to teach family principles; to show us how the family is supposed to reflect God's relationship with us.)

What are the strengths of this family? (Wealth, forgiveness, a wise father.)

What are the weaknesses of this family? (Father may not have given the older son enough recognition; there was jealousy; the older son was not compassionate about his brother; the father may have been too generous.)

What do you think Jesus is trying to teach us about God's family? (How much our heavenly Father unconditionally loves us, God will always take us back. The family on earth is to reflect His family in heaven.)

❸ A Strong Family Is within Reach

Objective:
To look at six strengths of strong families (15 minutes).

Read the following excerpt by Chuck Swindoll:

My research confirms two findings: 1. A fulfilling and happy family is as strong today as it was fifty years ago—maybe even stronger, and 2. effective family life does not just happen; it is the result of deliberate intention, determination and practice. . . . Not much research is done on strong, happy families. Most professional authorities focus their attention on families that are fractured by internal struggles.

Professor Nick Stinnett is an exception. Dr. Stinnett . . . launched a fascinating "family strengths research project." . . . His study included strong black families as well as white, strong ethnic families, and strong single-parent families. . . . There was only one criterion for being included in the sample of strong families: the families had to rate themselves very high in marriage happiness and in their satisfaction in parent-child relationships. . . . The goals? Very simply, to discover what makes families strong.

Dr. Stinnett found six main qualities in strong families. Strong families:
- are committed to the family
- spend time together
- have good family communication
- express appreciation to each other

Strong families are committed to the family. . . . spend time together. . . . have good family communication. . . . express appreciation. . . .

- **have a spiritual commitment**
- **and are able to solve problems in a crisis.**[3]

Direct attention to the six banners (each with one of the six characteristics of a strong family on it) you have taped around the room. Divide the group into six teams, so there is an equal number of participants sitting under each banner. Give each team this assignment: **Your pastor will be giving a series of sermons talking about strong family life. He wants your group to help him come up with practical, realistic, but challenging ideas for how the family characteristic on your banner can be enhanced.** Have the teams write their ideas on the bottom part of their banner.

The next step will give people a chance to appreciate the creative ideas of other teams. Use the following ideas should any team need some priming. These strengths complement each other, so it's natural that some of them appear under more than one characteristic.

Strong families are committed to the family. (Meet as a family on a weekly basis. Place a priority on taking time to do fun things together as a family. Mom and Dad should make it a point to keep their relationship solid. Parents should talk over important issues with the family in light of what certain decisions might mean for the family. Work less. Divide up family responsibilities so one person doesn't carry too much of the load.)

Strong families spend time together. (Meet as a family on a weekly basis. Mom and Dad schedule special time with each child each week. Take family vacations. Enjoy meals together as much as possible. Take the phone off the hook during meals. Have a game night each week. Plan fun days with the kids in charge, giving them a budget.)

Strong families have good family communication. (Meet as a family on a weekly basis. Mom and Dad schedule special time with each child each week. Develop an environment where the family focuses on solutions to problems. Emphasize time spent together interacting with less time in front of the tube. Talk with—not at—each other.)

Strong families express appreciation to each other. (Declare a "special person" day once a month, rotating it between all family members; the person gets a special meal and everyone says one positive thing about him or her.

Mom and Dad write love letters to the children. Siblings attend each other's athletic, music, and drama performances and provide moral support. Ask for the children's help when doing an important task.)

Strong families have a spiritual commitment. (Mom and Dad make it a habit to pray with each child at bedtime. Have devotions at dinner time. Attend church together. Talk about important issues together in light of spiritual realities.)

Strong families are able to solve problems in a crisis. (Make the children part of the decision-making process. Have them work with parents in establishing rules. Parents make it a point not to deal with hard issues while they are feeling emotionally charged. Discuss potential crisis situations before they occur. Emphasize solutions; don't blame. Learn what's normal and what's a crisis.)

❹ How Does My Family Measure Up?

Objective:
To give participants an opportunity to spend some time evaluating their own families (10 minutes).

After the completed banners have been rehung, distribute copies of "Looking at the Strength of Our Family" (RS-8C) and have the participants fill it out alone.

Take a look at your family and evaluate to determine where it needs strengthening. Indicate under the column "I say" how strong you think that characteristic is in your family. Write down what you think your children might say under their column. For ideas on how to make your family stronger, walk around the room looking at the suggestions provided on the banners of the other characteristics of strong families.

Let the banners serve as an "Idea Fair" to help the parents. Have them write ideas in the third column of the work sheet.

Conclude the session in prayer.

Notes:

1. Tony Evans, "Home and Alone," *Urban Family*, Fall 1993, 10.

2. Steven Johnson and Colin McMahon, "Sixty-One Young Victims Leave Behind a Trail of Anger, Abuse, and Blame," *Chicago Tribune*, January 2, 1994, 6.

3. Chuck Swindoll, *The Strong Family* (Portland, Ore.: Multnomah Press, 1991), 13, 14.

Habits of Effective Parents

9

Session Aim:
To help parents contrast effective and ineffective parenting techniques.

Have you thought about where you picked up your parenting habits? Most of us either mimic the techniques our parents used with us or try to do the opposite if we did not like how they raised us. If we had strict parents, we may have the tendency to be lenient. If they gave us lots of room to make our own mistakes, we may hold our children tightly to protect them from error.

For better or worse, parenting habits can be influenced by reading books and magazines, seeing a television special, or even by public opinion. For instance, in these days the disapproval of others keeps many parents from spanking their children, whether or not they have consciously evaluated the practice.

Regardless of where the habits originated, all parents have particular behaviors that are repeated. Some are good for children, making them secure and emotionally healthy. Others can cause hurt and can contribute to poor self-esteem, rebellion, laziness, and sometimes violence in our children.

It is easy to fall into patterns that don't help us accomplish the important work of raising our kids. This session will encourage habits that help children develop into the young men and women that God wants them to be.

Gaining a new habit or shaking an old one does not happen quickly.

Getting Ready

Scriptures:

Galatians 6:7-10; Deuteronomy 6:6, 7; Proverbs 10:19; 22:6; II Chronicles 1:11, 12; Colossians 3:21; James 1:19; I Corinthians 12:12; I Thessalonians 5:23.

1. Make enough copies for everyone of "If I Sow . . . I Will Reap" (RS-9A), "Habits of Effective Christian Parents" (RS-9B), and "Effective Parenting Evaluation" (RS-9C).
2. Make an extra copy of "If I Sow . . . I Will Reap" (RS-9A) and cut it into strips with one statement on each strip. Do the same with additional copies of the resource sheet as needed so that you will have enough strips to give one to each parent.
3. A whistle or bell that can get the attention of all even when they are making noise.

❶ Oh Yeah! I Know All about Habits

Objective:

To examine and define habits (10 minutes).

Gaining a new habit or shaking an old one does not happen quickly. But because habits are learned, they can be unlearned. It takes time and commitment. Leadership expert, Stephen Covey, tells us that habits are developed at the intersection of desire, skill, and knowledge.[1]

On the board, draw three intersecting circles as shown below. Label one circle "Desire," another "Skills," and the third "Knowledge." At the intersection of the three, write in big letters, "HABITS."

Bad Habits I've Seen

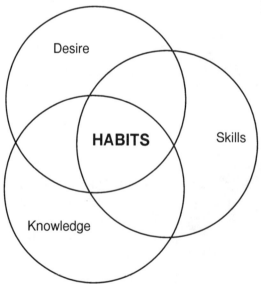

Then to the side write, "Bad Habits I've Seen." Have the group brainstorm about typical bad habits. (Biting nails, licking lips, smacking lips, making noises while reading.) Ask: **Do people who bite their nails have the knowledge,**

64

*S*ow *a thought, reap an action; sow an action, reap a habit; sow a habit, reap a character; sow a character, reap a destiny."*

skill, or the desire to do it? (All three, plus time are the ingredients for the development of a habit.)

Name a habit you wish your children *would* **develop.** Have fun with this. (Cleaning up their rooms, doing their school work without being told, developing interests in other things besides television and video games, asking how they can help, refilling the gas tank.)

Does your son or daughter have the skill to begin the new behavior you'd like to encourage? (Probably.) **The knowledge?** (Good chance.) **The desire?** (Aha! That's probably the missing ingredient.)

Now let's list a few negative parenting habits that your children might say *you* **have.** (Not listening, yelling too much, embarrassing them in front of their friends, not keeping track of their schedules, etc.) Discuss two or three of these habits and ask whoever named them whether their children would say that they as parents have the skill to change the habit . . . the knowledge . . . and the desire.

Possibly you don't agree with your sons or daughters that the habits they wish you would change are all that important, but are there habits you would like to change? Or more importantly, are there parenting skills you would like to learn or strengthen if you knew that they would help your kids grow up better? In this session, we will examine our parenting habits and behaviors and determine if the habit should be added to our parenting tool box or thrown away.

❷ We Reap What We Sow

Objective:
To consider the benefit of developing positive parenting habits (10-15 minutes).

There is a popular maxim that says, **"Sow a thought, reap an action; sow an action, reap a habit; sow a habit, reap a character; sow a character, reap a destiny."**

Ask a volunteer to read Galatians 6:7-10, and discuss it as a biblical foundation for the truth of the previous maxim.

Make sure everyone has a blank sheet of paper and a pen or pencil. Then let each person pick a slip of paper that you cut up from "If I Sow . . . I Will Reap" (RS-9A.) (This resource sheet is based on I Corinthians 13, the "love chapter.")

Have group members find partners and interview the partner to complete the statement on their slips. They should record the partner's answer on their blank sheet of paper. When one partner has solicited the other partner's response,

Our calling as parents is to guide our children, supplying them with what they need in order to be effective, godly men and women.

they should switch so that both partners get a chance to offer an answer.

Give the partners only one minute to come up with answers before you blow the whistle or ring the bell indicating that they should form new pairs. Repeat this four or five times depending on the amount of time you have for your session. Distribute a copy of the resource to each person and encourage the group members to complete this resource sheet on their own.

❸ What Are Habits of Effective Christian Parenting?

Objective:
To suggest habits of effectiveness and apply them to Christian parenting (20 minutes).

Business guru, Stephen Covey, has written a best-selling book, *The Seven Habits of Highly Effective People*,[2] that has helped millions of people, and his ideas are compatible with Christian principles. Covey argues for lives built upon a "character" ethic with attributes such as hard work, integrity, fairness, honesty, faith, commitment, sincerity, compassion, etc.

The seven habits he recommends came from studying effective people, men and women who get the job done without burning out themselves or those close to them.

That's a key for parenting. God has given us our children, a great gift. Our family is of primary importance. Our calling as parents is to guide our children, supplying them with what they need in order to be effective, godly men and women. We cannot do it if we are burning ourselves out or alienating our children. We need to develop habits of effectiveness in our own lives.

Effectiveness is different than efficiency. Parents sometimes want a quick fix for their family, a magic potion. There is no such thing. Being a healthy family is never efficient. Parenting is hard work and takes time.

Hand out the work sheet, "Habits of Effective Christian Parents" (RS-9B). Divide into small groups of two or three people per group and assign each group one or two principles to discuss in light of the following questions. Write these questions on the board:

A. How could this habit help someone become a more effective parent?
B. How might the lack of this habit chase our children into the arms of a waiting culture?

C. **Why might it be hard to develop this habit?**

D. **What skills and knowledge are needed to develop this habit?**

After a few minutes, reconvene the large group and have the small groups share their responses. If there are any questions, here are possible responses. (The letters below correspond to the questions you have written on the board.)

1. **Be proactive.**

   (A. It might help parents slow down and be more reflective about their actions and reactions to things.

   B. Parents who base everything on moods, feelings, and circumstances instead of biblical values tend to provide a less stable home environment.

   C. Behavior based on values might not be as much fun because it requires discipline and intentional parenting.

   D. Parents need to know what they believe, how to make choices, and understand the consequences of various behaviors.)

2. **Begin with the end in mind.**

   (A. If parents know what they want to build into their children's lives, they have the makings of a plan.

   B. Without a plan, everything becomes hit or miss depending on the mood or feeling. Kids might not feel consistency, progress, or a sense of determination on the part of the parent.

   C. Some people feel it is unholy or lacking in faith to plan ahead. Once you have a plan, there is a sense of obligation to work it. Parents sometimes don't want to feel obligated.

   D. Parents need to know how to think about the future, how to pray and seek God's will, and what is important for a child to grow up well.)

3. **Put first things first.**

   (A. By putting first things first, parents begin to live out the parenting plans they have developed. They'll do those things that are important, that help their children grow within a consistent environment.

   B. Kids going to the streets often is the result of parents who fail to make parenting their first priority. Everything else is more important.

   C. We have developed habits of doing the unimportant

first. Sometimes the unimportant stuff in our lives looks like a lot more fun than the daily call to be a good parent.

D. Might need to develop good time management and have someone hold me accountable to it.)

4. **Think win/win.**

(A. It forces parents to listen to their child's point of view. The parent can't win and the child can't win unless they are listening to each other express needs.

B. Too many kids are in win/lose situations. The parents always have to be right. When in that kind of an environment, the children look elsewhere for support.

C. Pride, stubbornness, and a warped sense of what it means to be a parent stands in the way of a parent trying to interact with his or her child.

D. Need listening and negotiating skills.)

5. **Seek first to understand . . . then be understood.**

(A. Listening is foundational. How can a parent minister to his or her child if the parent doesn't understand what is going on in the child's life?

B. Kids will look for others who will listen to them. Parents who want to be understood before they listen are an "argument waiting to happen."

C. We live in a world that places a high premium on verbal skills and not enough emphasis on listening. When we listen, we might not like what we hear.

D. Parents need to learn how to reflect back to their children the feeling and content of the children's messages. This enables the parents to know whether they have heard the kids correctly.)

6. **Synergy.**

(A. When parents value the uniqueness of everyone in the family, they recognize the importance of the differences all bring to the home. Not everyone has to be a clone. The family begins to take responsibility for each other.

B. Parents who want their kids to fit a preconceived mold fail to recognize the value of differences and sometimes unknowingly encourage kids to rebel.

C. Where there are differences, things can get a bit chaotic. A parent who places a high value on "smooth sailing" at all times is going to struggle with this.

D. Need to understand the value of a family working

together as a team. Need to have empathy and have a willingness to love the uniqueness of each son or daughter.)

7. Sharpen the saw.
(A. This is the habit of self-renewal. One just can't keep giving and giving without getting his or her "batteries" charged.

B. Parents who aren't renewed are prone to irritability, anger, bouts of depression, etc.

C. In some circles, taking care of yourself is considered a sign of selfishness. In some families, there isn't a lot of time for self-renewal.

D. People need self-evaluative skills that will force them to ask the hard questions about whether or not they are striking a good balance in their lives.)

❹ Self-Examination

Objective:
To have parents evaluate themselves in light of the seven principles of effective parenting and to determine at least one specific action to take within the next week (5-15 minutes).

Distribute copies of the "Effective Parenting Evaluation" (RS-9C) and ask the parents to evaluate themselves.

If time allows, encourage the participants to write a short-term goal statement addressing how they might strengthen those areas where their parenting habits are weakest.

To close, encourage husbands and wives to pray for one another concerning their areas of need. Parents who are present without a spouse can be teamed in twos or threes—men with men and women with women as much as possible.

Notes:

1. Stephen R. Covey, *The Seven Habits of Highly Effective People: Restoring the Character Ethic* (New York: Simon and Schuster, 1989).
2. Ibid.

Do Not "Exasperate" Our Kids

10

Session Aim:
To help parents begin to
develop habits of effective
Christian parenting.

1. I can do anything I please.

2. I am the boss.

3. I am always right.

4. Children have no say in setting rules.

5. My viewpoint is the only one that counts.

6. My word is final.

Mark Twain gave this humorous advice about children: "When they turn twelve, put 'em in a barrel and feed 'em through that little hole. When they turn sixteen, plug up the hole!"

Too often young people have succeeded in becoming the fingernails on the blackboard of their parents' lives. On the other hand, many parents have succeeded in exasperating their offspring. In some cases, this has given birth to a full-blown rebellion.

The family is the first line of defense for helping young people deal with a violent culture. But what if the family structure is impaired in some way? What if parents use communication strategies that, "don't work, won't work, and shouldn't work," but insist on using them anyway? Where will young people turn?

Hopefully, they will turn to other significant adults. But if other caring adults are not present, the streets have open arms. The young person will find within those arms negative peer influence, a warped culture, gang activity, and probably violence. We've got to keep our kids out of the streets!

The family is the first line of defense for helping young people deal with a violent culture.

Getting Ready:

Scriptures:
Ephesians 6:1-4;
Eccelsiates 1:9.

1. Make enough copies for everyone of "The Dirty Dozen: Parenting Strategies for an Unhappy Family" (RS-10A) and "Clarifying the Parenting Issues" (RS-10B).
2. On separate 3 x 5 card, write out the three skit scenarios in Step 1 (see page 72).
3. Create signs to post around the room with the following words on them:
   NEVER, EVER
   MY KIDS WOULD'SAY I DO IT ALL THE TIME
   SOMETIMES, MORE THAN I'D LIKE TO ADMIT
   I THINK IT A LOT, BUT I USUALLY DON'T ACT ON IT
   UH-OH! THAT'S ME.
   SOUNDS A LOT LIKE MY NEIGHBOR
4. Copy the following questions on the board and, if possible, cover them until they are needed in Step 3 see page 73).
   • Can you think of a reason why a parent might justify using this strategy?
   • When parents use this strategy, what is the usual reaction of children?
   • How could following this strategy be considered a violent act?
5. Optional: Small prize for the group who includes the most strategies from "The Dirty Dozen" in their skit in Step 1.

❶ We're So Bad . . . We Could Be a Sitcom

Objective:
To identify twelve parenting strategies that don't work (10-15 minutes).

Hand out the resource sheet, "The Dirty Dozen: Parenting Strategies for an Unhappy Family" (RS-10A). Ask volunteers to read aloud one "Strategy" at a time.

Allow the parents a few moments to look over the sheet as you explain that these are typical behaviors engaged in by some parents. Chances are everyone in the room has done one or more of the activities listed. These strategies have proven to be quite toxic in family relationships. The result is that family members, "don't trust, don't talk, don't resolve problems" and look elsewhere for meaning and purpose. Many children who develop at-risk behaviors will tell you these are strategies that have chased them into the street.

Sometimes parents say that their children push them or even force them into acting in negative ways at times. There is a fundamental rule that governs human relationships: "The only person I can control in a relationship is me." This means, I still have the freedom to

choose appropriate responses no matter what my child does.

Write on the board: "The only person I can control in a relationship is me." Ask the group if they agree with this statement.

Have the participants form three groups. Announce that we have just formed the "Unhappy Family Players." Each group will act out one of the following scenarios using as many of the "Dirty Dozen" principles as possible. Give each group one of the 3 x 5 cards with one of the following scenarios written on it:

Skit 1: Act out a typical scene between parents and children discussing a home situation where they disagree.

Skit 2: Act out a group of kids sitting around talking about their parents who use these strategies. Zero in on what they feel kids' honest reactions to these strategies might be.

Skit 3: Act out a group of parents defending their use of one or more of the "Dirty Dozen."

After the skits are performed for the whole group, take a vote on which skit used the most "Dirty Dozen" strategies. Optional: Give each member of the winning cast a small prize.

Have the parents stay in the same three groups for the next activity.

❷ Don't Exasperate Them

Objective:
To discover what the Bible says about aggravating our children (10 minutes).

Read Ephesians 6:1-3. Ask: **How many of you hope and pray that your children will take this commandment to heart?** Ask for a show of hands. Most hands should go up.

Before reading verse four, explain: **The next verse is one your kids are hoping and praying your will take to heart!** Read verse four aloud.

Group one to make a list of things their parents did to aggravate them.

Group two to make a list of things their kids would say they do to cause aggravation.

Group three to make a list of kids' responses when aggravated by their parents.

Bring the three groups together again, and have them share their lists.

❸ A Closer Look

Objective:
To help parents identify their responses and discuss possible outcomes of using typical parenting strategies (15 minutes).

Read aloud and place the six signs around the room that you made before the session. Instruct the group that you will be reading the "Dirty Dozen" one at a time. As you do so, they should go to the sign that best describes their response. Once a group gathers under the sign, have them answer the three questions that you wrote on the board before group time.

- **Can you think of a reason why a parent might justify using this strategy?**
- **When parents use this strategy, what is the usual reaction of children?**
- **How could following this strategy be considered a violent act?**

❹ What Do We Know about Kids and What They Like?

Objective:
To review basic issues regarding kids and parenting (10-20 minutes).

Parents sometimes act the way they do because they have quit being students of their children and their culture. Many people have quit growing. Here's an easy true/false test that can help clarify some important issues.

Pass out "Clarifying the Parenting Issues" (RS-10B). Give parents time to indicate true or false to the statements on the resource sheet. After they have finished, go over the statements while offering the following input. As time allows, discuss each one.

1. Kids want a relationship with their parents. (*True.* Kids want parents to be available. But they don't want to be embarrassed by their parents. So, even though kids love to be able to talk to Mom and/or Dad about important issues, they sometimes behave cautiously. As kids grow older, the relationship needs to redefine itself.)

2. Rules without relationship leads to rebellion. (*True.* Think of a time when you had a rule imposed upon you. How did you react? Kids like to give their input and feel like they've had a stake in the decision making. Parents need to build relationships with their kids.)

3. Times have changed so much. Everything my kid is going through is different than what I faced. (*False.* Kids are growing up in a different world, but the most critical things don't change. As Ecclesiastes 1:9 says, "there is nothing new under the sun." You can still understand what it feels like to be gossiped about, not be picked for a game, or to be apprehensive about relationships. Circumstances change. Feelings don't. Try to remember the feelings of childhood and adolescence.)

4. Choose your battles wisely or you'll be battling all the time. (*True.* Kids can push your button in 101 ways. Save the battle gear for the stuff that really matters.)

5. Kids are impressed when you say "When I was your age. . . ." (*False.* Kids are no more impressed when you say that than you were when your parents said the same to you.)

6. Kids will react better if they feel supported before being challenged. (*True.* Kids need to feel that they have a safe, secure, home base. Support your kids emotionally and you'll be able to challenge them in the important areas.)

7. Kids are under so much pressure, they don't need an environment filled with consequences. (*False.* Kids are under a lot of pressure because they grow up not knowing what real consequences are. However, try to make consequences naturally or logically related to the behavior so the kids will learn from their mistakes.)

8. Kids think faith is stupid. (*False.* Kids want a real faith, but it has got to be their faith. God has children, not grandchildren. As children become older, they cannot ride along on the coattails of your faith. Help your kids develop faith by modeling a godly lifestyle and by making faith a natural part of your life.)

9. The world is such a scary place that parents need to be especially strict with their kids. (*False.* Being overly strict can cause kids to rebel. Overly strict parents don't involve children in the decision-making process. The result is that the rules established appear arbitrary and unfair. Unless you plan on making every decision for your child the rest of his or her life you need to equip him or her to do it. Overly strict parents don't help their children develop an "internal" locus of decision making.)

10. The world is a scary place, so parents shouldn't add to it by making their kids afraid of them. Parents should avoid making any rules. (*False.* Your job is to prepare kids to live life. But because the world is a scary place, it's important that children are prepared for it every step of the way before they face adult responsibilities. Permissiveness is never a good strategy.)

Children need to understand that Mom and Dad aren't always going to be around to save them.

11. Kids are more mature these days. (*False*. They know more. They are more sophisticated and develop physically at a younger age, but that's not the same as wise maturity. Some adults want to think their children are mature because it is an excuse to back out of their parenting responsibilities, but kids are kids. Let's never forget that. Why do so many adults want to rob kids of a childhood? Kids know a lot more about a lot of things. But do they have the tools to deal with it all? The answer is usually NO.)

12. This is a new day and age. Kids don't need a dad. (*False*. Research clearly demonstrates that kids without a father struggle more than those from two-parent families. That doesn't mean they can't make it, but it is tougher for them.)

13. It's impossible for a single parent to raise a healthy child these days. (*False*. Single parents can and will continue to do a commendable job of child-rearing. The best scenario is a home with both a mom and dad who love one another. However, with the support of other adults, a single parent can provide the necessary resources spiritually, emotionally, and physically for a child to grow up healthy.)

14. There are kids who need a "tougher" kind of love. (*True*. "Tough Love" is a nationwide program that helps parents deal with children who are very strong-willed, habitually disobedient, and who don't respond well to normal disciplinary actions. These young people establish a long history of irresponsible behavior. Parents are urged to take a very strong stand against tremendously immature and destructive behavior. However, make sure you aren't trying to apply tough love techniques to a situation that doesn't need it or you could worsen the situation.)

15. It's okay to rescue children from their own mistakes. (*False*. Too many parents spend too much time trying to "rescue" their children from natural and logical consequences of their behavior. Children need to understand that Mom and Dad aren't always going to be around to save them. This is a scary world. Kids who are looking to someone else to face it for them won't develop the life skills necessary to deal with the wide variety of experiences and choices ahead of them.)

Conclude the session by having the participants team up with partners where they will each identify one of the "parenting issues" that they find most challenging and share why. Then they can pray for each other.

Parents, WE Can Do It!

11

Session Aim:
To help parents teach their children how to evaluate and make wise, godly choices, which will keep them from destructive paths.

Our culture loves gimmicks and slogans. We believe any problem can be solved with a first-rate marketing campaign, a sparkling image, and a well-chosen word. Garbage! They may be well intended, but they lack substance.

Do you believe guns will disappear from the street if we offer a "guns for sneakers" program? Do you believe that "Just say No!" to drugs really works? It may have some value in deglamorizing drugs, but life is too complex for it to have much impact on users.

It is good to hear anti-violence raps and star basketball players encourage our kids to "Work hard, don't be afraid to sweat for what you want, you can do it if you choose to do it." But positive media campaigns are useful only if they are part of a larger strategy . . . the strategy of the home.

Parents can teach their children to think about the consequences of their actions before a mistake is made. They are able to give guidelines to assist their children in understanding how to make wise choices. Parents can also help form their child's conscience.

If we need a slogan, let it be, "Parents, WE can help our kids do it!"

Parents can teach their children to think about the consequences of their actions before a mistake is made.

Getting Ready

Scriptures:
Matthew 7:13, 14;
Romans 1:20.

1. Photocopy enough copies of "Consequences" (RS-11A) and "What I Want to Build into My Child" (RS-11B).
2. Prepare large sheets of newsprint or butcher paper to cover table tops. (The number of tables depends on the size of your group. Make sure everyone can fit around a table. If tables are not available, people can work on the floor, or the sheets can be taped to the wall). Bring a sufficient number of crayons or colored markers for everyone to use. Ahead of time draw a path (starting at one end of the paper) that quickly divides into a straight narrow path and a broad winding path. This is for use in Step 2.

❶ Just Say "No!"

Objective:
To examine the ineffectiveness of popular slogans to help kids avoid trouble (5-10 minutes).

Ask participants these questions, soliciting their responses by a show of hands.

- **How many of you want your child to resist negative peer pressure?**
- **How many of you want your child to avoid gang involvement?**
- **How many of you don't want your child to be a victim of violence?**
- **How many of you don't want your child carrying a gun?**
- **How many of you don't want your child fighting?**
- **How many of you don't want your child watching violent movies?**
- **How many of you don't want your children following the advice of the "gangsta" rappers or heavy metal performers?**

Look the participants in the eye and tell them, **All you have to do to keep your children from these things is to tell them one thing, and everything will be okay. Ready? The magic formula . . . tell your children to "Just say No!" That's all you have to do.**

Pause for about a minute as you look from one person to the other. (It will seem like an eternity, but stretch it out as long as you can.)

Since the early '80s we have been teaching kids to say "no!" Has it been effective? The statistics report that sexually transmitted diseases,[1] teen pregnancy, and violent crimes have all increased dramatically.[2] Drug

rug use appears to be dropping among younger, African-American, urban children . . . due to its bitter consequences. . . .

usage is also terribly high and still rising among most teenagers. (Ironically, *Newsweek* magazine recently reported that drug use appears to be dropping among younger, African-American, urban children—not because of slogans or anti-drug programs, due to its bitter consequences in their own homes and neighborhoods.[3])

What are some of the good things the slogan campaigns have done? (The campaigns get the majority of the public to become aware of the problem. They help younger kids become aware and exposed to warnings at an early age. It's good to see positive comments in the media.)

What is ineffective about these positive slogan campaigns? (A person may give lip service to something that does not come from the heart. When a person says "no," he or she could mean "maybe," or talk to me a little more about what you have in mind and I might say "yes." These kind of campaigns usually don't work with older children.)

Make two columns on the board. Label one column NO; the other YES. Record the group's responses to the following questions in the appropriate column.

What do you want your children to say "no" to? Think about the lessons we have already covered and include those ideas. (We want our children to say "no" to garbage in media, violent activity, premarital sex, materialism, secularism, gangs, drugs, etc.) Record the participants' responses on the board.

What are some of the negative consequences of saying "no"? (Peer problems, loneliness, getting beat up for convictions, ridicule, etc.)

What do you want your children to say "yes" to? (Healthy recreational programs, family relationships, good music and entertainment, family, school, Jesus Christ, positive peer pressure, etc.).

Are there any consequences to this behavior? (Feeling good about one's self. Others may want to follow you. Eternal life.)

Leave these responses on the board.

Our kids need to learn to say "no!" and they need to understand the rewards of saying "yes!"

❷ Finding the Narrow Path

Objective:
To help parents inform their children what the narrow path is and how to get on it (15 minutes).

Have everyone turn to Matthew 7:13, 14 as you read the verses aloud: **"Enter through the narrow gate. For wide is the gate and broad is the road that leads to destruction, and many enter through it. But small is the gate and narrow the road that leads to life, and only a few find it."**

Is the NO column the wide or narrow road? (Obviously, it is the wider road.)

Invite the group members to gather around the large sheets of newsprint (on tables, floor, or walls). Provide crayons or colored markers. Have people within each group number off as "1" or "2." Ask all the number "1s" to draw something along the narrow path that they would like their kids to say "yes" to. Have all number "2s" draw something along the broad path that might entice a young person to take that way. Warn the groups that they have only five minutes for their creation.

When the time is up, encourage everyone to note what others have drawn. Some explanation may be in order.

Why do so many young people choose the broad path? (There is a lot of company on this way. It's the popular way. While the things on this path aren't good for you, they provide short-term pleasure.)

Why does the narrow path have only a few people on it? (To follow this road, one must make a choice. Because it is narrow, it is easier to get off the path, therefore it requires a real commitment. It's a lonelier road. Even before you get on it, this road looks harder and less fun.)

As Christian parents we want our kids on the narrow road. Our desire is for our children to experience "life" as God defines it. Slogans and gimmicks aren't enough to keep them walking along the narrow path.

How would you describe a "narrow path" lifestyle? (It's a pattern of life in which we choose godly behavior. It's having sufficient faith to keep our eyes focused on Jesus.)

What skills are necessary to make "narrow path" lifestyle decisions? (A good conscience. Courage to follow through on decisions. Sufficient information to make good decisions. Being able to think beforehand and evaluate the consequences of one's behavior.)

Our kids need to learn to say "no!" and they need to understand the rewards of saying "yes!" However, they also need to know why they are making those decisions and to have the skills necessary to choose the better way. To live this kind of life, our youth must have faith that will take them through some hard times. Courage is essential to continue walking along the path when others are not. Our kids need to know that saying "no" is just one strategy for a narrow road lifestyle.

❸ Teaching "Narrow Path" Living

Objective:
To help parents understand that "narrow path" living is a long process and requires consistent modeling (10 minutes).

Parents cannot be involved intimately with every detail of their children's lives. However, as William Kilpatrick writes in *Why Johnny Can't Tell Right from Wrong:*

> Parents need to be working toward the creation of what Louis Sullivan, the secretary of health and human services, calls a "Culture of Character." As Sullivan says, "A new culture of character in America nurtured by strengthened families and communities, would do much to alleviate the alienation, isolation and despair that fuel teen pregnancy, violence, drug and alcohol abuse and other social problems afflicting us. . . . Study after study has shown that children who are raised in an environment of strong values tend to thrive in every sense.[4]

Explore with the parents how one goes about creating a "Culture of Character" that can be the launching pad for a "narrow road" lifestyle. To stimulate discussion, ask how successful the following approaches are:

- **Wishing it will happen.**
- **Hoping it will happen.**
- **Expecting others to do it for you.**
- **Forcing it into your children.**
- **Yelling it into your children.**
- **Letting kids figure it out for themselves.**

If these methods don't work—never have, never will—ask group members what will work.

There's an old maxim that says: "Give a man a fish and you'll feed him for a day. Teach him to fish and he'll eat for a lifetime." Longshoreman/philosopher Eric

We will not always be with our children, so it's wise to teach them certain things now.

Hoffer once said, "In times of change, learners inherit the earth, while the learned find themselves beautifully equipped to deal with a world that no longer exists."

Ask the group to discuss the advantages of teaching our children "how to fish" and encouraging them to become learners. List their responses on the board. (It has long-term benefits. We will not always be with our children, so it's wise to teach them certain things now. Children need to learn how to handle situations in life. Children can become independent of us.)

What does teaching our children to fish and encouraging them to become learners mean in terms of parental commitment? (We have to be committed to teaching the principles, allowing experiences so they can learn, letting go, and taking risks.)

What keeps parents away from this kind of an approach? (It's time consuming. It takes a commitment. It can feel risky. We may not know how to do it.)

Now, ask parents to think back to the time when they learned to ride a bike. Ask them to describe elements of that learning experience. Write them on the board. This list should include things like:

> (• There was someone there to help me.
> • I made a lot of mistakes.
> • I learned from my mistakes.
> • I tried different techniques until I found one that worked.
> • It was hard.
> • I got hurt.
> • Once I learned, I never forgot.
> • I almost did it, but then I fell.
> • Wobbly was good enough at first.
> • I gained confidence to try without help.)

How is learning to ride a bike similar to teaching our children how to choose a "narrow road" lifestyle and saying "no" to negative pressures? (The responses should be similar to our learning to ride a bike experience noted above.)

Teaching our children to walk the narrow path is the same way. We can't just hope they'll do it. We can't expect them to know how. Walking through the mine-

field of our culture and choosing the narrow way will require:

- **A mentor (preferably Mom and Dad).**
- **Willingness to take risks to learn how to make decisions.**
- **A lot of mistakes and learning from those mistakes.**
- **Uncertainty tempered with faith.**
- **Hurt.**
- **Prayer.**
- **A firm hand.**
- **Someone to be there when you fall.**
- **A ton of encouragement.**

❹ "Narrow Path" Living and Consequences

Objective:
To think through the value of establishing consequences for our children's actions (10 minutes).

Write the word CONSEQUENCES on the board. Explain to the group that an important aspect of teaching our kids to walk the narrow path includes not rescuing them from the consequences of their actions unless those consequences are so dire that we would be acting irresponsibly.

Under the word CONSEQUENCES write on the left NATURAL and on the right LOGICAL. **What are the natural results of an action?** (The consequences that arise from the behavior. For instance, if you turn the wrong way when riding a bicycle, you may lose your balance, fall off, and hurt yourself. When you forget your lunch at home, you go hungry during the lunch hour. When you don't study for a test, you risk failure.)

What are logical consequences? (They are results that need to be imposed when the natural consequences aren't obvious.)

Under LOGICAL write the words Related, Respectful, Revealed, Reasonable. **According to Jane Nelsen in her book *Positive Discipline*,[5] a good logical consequence is related to the incident, it respects the child, if possible it is revealed ahead of time (negotiated with child), and it is reasonable (teaches rather than punishes).**

For example, if a child is involved in a fight with another child, he or she will suffer whatever bruises or cuts result from the fight (natural consequence). But in addition, he or she has to pay for the ripped jacket of the other person (logical consequence).

We are witnessing in America the most terrifying thing that could happen to a society—the death of conscience.

What do you think will happen to children who are not raised in a consequential environment? (They will think they are able to do anything and never have to suffer for it. They think parents or someone will always bail them out, and they will never learn responsibility for their own actions.)

What will happen to children who find themselves in an environment where parents want to use consequences to punish rather than teach? (The children will experience anger, frustration, rebellion, etc. There will be frequent negative confrontations, etc.)

Give each person the handout entitled, "Consequences" (RS-11A). Encourage everyone to study it at home as a further resource for understanding how various consequences relate to parenting.

❺ Knowing Right from Wrong

Objective:
To explore ways of nurturing the conscience of young people (5-15 minutes).

Charles Colson paid a stiff penalty for his choices. He was a major player in the Nixon White House scandal, commonly known as "Watergate." At the time, he felt he was above the law. As a result, he went to prison. Now, he heads a ministry to prison inmates. At the dedication of the Focus on the Family building in Colorado Springs, Colson made these remarks about conscience.

We are witnessing in America the most terrifying thing that could happen to a society—the death of conscience. . . . Where does conscience come from? It is something God gave us at birth, but it has to be cultivated. . . .

Aristotle said virtue consists of not merely knowing what is right, but also in having the will to do what is right, and the will is trained by practice, by choosing to do right continually until it becomes a habit. . . .

That is why what is happening to the family today is so dangerous. Adults are spending 40 percent less time with their kids than their parents spent with them. . . .

Because these parents are not cultivating conscience in their children we are producing a generation of 12 year olds who are roaming the streets with pistols, shooting one another.

The second way in which conscience is cultivated is through moral consensus—the values and moral truth a society shares and the rules people agree to live by. . . .

Presently, our society is walking down a dangerous path where there are no moral values, no absolute truth that tells us how we should live.[6]

Ask for a show of hands on how many believe violence is a result of people who never learned right from wrong and how many believe it is a result of people who know the difference, but choose to ignore what is right.

This is an interesting, ongoing debate. We know that too many young people haven't had the love, care, and nurture necessary to fully cultivate their sense of right and wrong. Their consciences are undeveloped and sputtering along. However, that's not the last word on the issue.

Have someone read Romans 1:20, then comment: **So even with a conscience that hasn't been cultivated, there is no excuse for sin. We may find some explanations, but there are no excuses.**

Ask the participants to form a "pinwheel" by dividing the group into two equal parts. Have one part form a circle with their chairs facing outward. Have the other group form a circle around the first circle with their chairs facing inward. They should be opposite someone from the other group. For each question you read, have the participants in the outer circle move one chair to the right in order to face a new partner. They can discuss the question until you call time and read a new question. Keep this moving quickly.

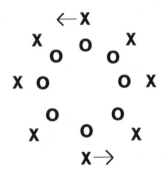

- **Is Colson right? Are there too many young people running around without a good sense of right and wrong?**
- **Do you think the violence in today's culture is a result of people who never learned right from wrong or because they chose to ignore what's right?**
- **Who helped you form your conscience?**
- **What did that person(s) do to cultivate your conscience?**
- **What are some of the things that are wrong in our**

culture that you want your children to know about?
- How will you teach your children that in a violent world there can be some very disastrous consequences to actions?
- What role does faith play in the development of conscience?

Before closing the session in prayer, ask the parents to prepare for the next session by completing "What I Want to Build into My Child" (RS-11B). Emphasize the importance of their finishing it before the next session and bringing it back next time. If there is time, allow them to begin it before closing. The purpose of the activity is to get parents thinking about their goals for their children and how they want to go about building certain qualities, beliefs, values, perceptions, and skills into their children's lives.

Close in prayer asking God to help each parent find time to prayerfully consider how to apply the material in this session. Also thank Him for parents who want to make a positive difference in their kids' lives.

Notes:

1. "Adolescence, 13-18," *Free to Be Family* (Washington, D.C.: Family Research Council, 1992), 77, 78.

2. William J. Bennett, *The Index of Leading Cultural Indicators* (New York: Simon and Schuster, 1994), 22, 23, 30, 31, 74, 75.

3. Carroll Bogert, "Good News on Drugs from the Inner City," *Newsweek*, February 14, 1994, 28, 29.

4. William Kilpatrick, *Why Johnny Can't Tell Right From Wrong: Moral Literacy and the Case for Character Education.* (New York: Simon and Schuster, 1992), 252.

5. Jane Nelsen, *Positive Discipline* (New York: Ballantine, 1987).

6. Chuck Colson, "Where Did Our Conscience Go?" *Focus on the Family* magazine, January 1994, 12, 13.

I Couldn't Help Myself!

12

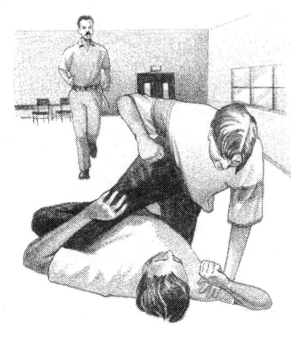

Session Aim:
To help parents see the need for a strong sense of right and wrong and to equip them to assist their children in developing one.

Remember the cartoon, "Tweety Bird and Sylvester"? The little old lady goes out, leaving behind her cherished pets, Sylvester the Cat and Tweety Bird, a canary. Sylvester is usually napping on the floor while Tweety Bird is singing in a cage.

At first all seems well. Then a miniature devil hops onto Sylvester's shoulder. It is dressed in red, with a pitchfork, long tail and horns. "Sylvester," the voice allures, "wouldn't you like to have Tweety Bird for lunch?" Before you know it, Sylvester is licking his chops.

Then another image hops onto Sylvester's other shoulder. This one is dressed like an angel, decked out in a white robe, with a halo and harp. "Now, Sylvester," the angel encourages, "you don't want to eat your friend Tweety Bird. How disappointed Granny will be to come home and find her Tweety Bird eaten by the cat."

In every episode, Sylvester ignores the angel and attempts to capture Tweety Bird. The bird always escapes in the nick of time while Sylvester ends up beaten, bitten, or badly wounded.

A profound message in a cartoon. God's way is always best. Satan's way always leads to destruction. This session will help us convey this lesson to our children.

God's way is always best. Satan's way always leads to destruction.

Getting Ready:

Scriptures:
Luke 14:25-34.

1. Photocopy "What I Want to Build into My Child" (RS-11B) from last week for group members who might have forgotten to bring it back.
2. Photocopy "Parenting Strategies (RS-12A) and "A Dialogue . . . Good Parenting at Work" (RS-12B). Make an extra copy of RS-12A. Both resources are two pages.
3. Cut up the extra copy of RS-12A for use in Step 3 (see page 88).
4. Before the session, contact a couple of parents and ask them to do a skit based on "A Dialogue . . . Good Parenting at Work" (RS-12B). Get copies of the skit to the "actors" before the session if possible. If they can't get together to rehearse the skit on their own, suggest that they come a half hour early to practice. They do not need to memorize their parts, just be familiar enough with them to read convincingly.
5. Write these questions on the board ahead of time for use in Step 1:
   - Is what you want to build into your child based upon principles from God's Word? Upon which ones?
   - When you think of the parenting task before you, how do you feel?
   - What do you need to start doing today to accomplish what you are setting out to do?
   - How can the Body of Christ help?

❶ What Will My Child Say about Me When I'm Ninety?

Objective:
To help parents begin to set goals for each child (5-10 minutes).

Break the group into small teams of two or three people each and have them read aloud their speech from "What I Want to Build into My Child" (RS-11B) that was assigned as preparation for this session. For those who may not have prepared, encourage them to share extemporaneously what they would like one of their children to say about them at their ninetieth birthday party.

When the team members have given their speeches, tell them to discuss with each other their plans for building specific things into the life of their children.

After the parents have finished discussing the questions on RS-11B, have them answer the questions you wrote on the board ahead of time. Allow a few volunteers to share their answers. Ask how the group members can help each other.

❷ By the Grace Of God, I Will . . .

Objective:
To discover the parallels between Jesus' comments about the cost of being a disciple and the challenges of being a good parent (5-10 minutes).

With the parents still in their separate teams, ask them to open their Bibles to Luke 14:25-34. Have everyone read it silently. Give each team an assignment based on the passage. If you have more than four teams, duplicate assignments as needed. If you have fewer than four groups assign more than one question to groups as needed.

Team 1: How is being a parent like "carrying the cross" and being Jesus' disciple? (For the sake of your child, you have to do things that you otherwise would not want to do. It is a heavy responsibility.)

Team 2: How was doing the take-home assignment like "building the tower"? (It's part of the process of counting the cost of raising a godly child. You have to add up the expense, it will cost you something. You need a firm foundation.)

Team 3: How was doing the take-home assignment like a king preparing for war? (We are preparing our kids for spiritual battle. We need a strategy and a plan and we need to gather the resources to accomplish the task.)

Team 4: How is a parent to avoid losing his or her saltiness? (By following God, staying on top of things, working hard, etc. Salt preserves food from decay, and we must resist corruption in our own lives and in the lives of our families.)

Reunite the group and have each team share the best of their findings.

❸ You Can Do It

Objective:
To show parents how they can start building into the lives of their children necessary perceptions and skills (15-20 minutes).

Before the group time, you should have cut apart a copy of "Parenting Strategies" (RS-12A). Divide up the twenty-two slips of strategies so that each class member gets about the same number, excluding the two people who will be doing the skit. They will get none. Point out that the numbers on the slips are for reference later and do not indicate the order used in the skit.

Explain that in a moment there will be a skit (see RS-12B) during which each group member is to watch for the particular strategies he or she has been given. Allow time for all group members to read over their slips of paper silently. Then tell them to listen and watch carefully for examples of their assigned strategies. Inform them that at the end of the dramatization they will share how they saw their strategies portrayed in the skit.

Explain that this dramatization is designed to share some realistic, doable, and necessary parenting strategies that will help equip their sons and daughters for living in a violent culture. Point out that although the child in this skit is a teenager, the strategies can be used with children of all ages. In fact, the sooner these principles are put to use, the more effective they will be overall.

The script for the skit is "A Dialogue . . . Good Parenting at Work" (RS-12B). The "actors" should have rehearsed it ahead of time. Ask them to perform it at this point.

❹ Learning from Each Other

Objective:
To identify helpful skills and attitudes for parents to use with their children (10-15 minutes).

Pass out additional complete copies of "Parenting Strategies" (RS-12A) as a reference for all the parents. Have parents share where they saw "their strategies" (the slips in their hands) at work.

Generate discussion by asking questions such as:

How could using these strategies in our homes help us in equipping our children to live in a violent world?

Do any of these strategies appear more necessary than others?

How might both the child and the parent feel after an interaction like this?

Have group members share about their successes in using these or similar strategies. Ask what other strategies they might use.

Some of the parents might suggest that the skit looks good on paper, but is unrealistic in the real world of their home. It's possible that some parents believe in a very strict, punitive approach to parenting. Do not get in a debate with them, but ask how the parenting strategies they are using are working and how their child is responding. Ask if they feel comfortable that it is preparing their child adequately to make his or her own decisions. Don't put the parents on the spot, just encourage thoughtful evaluation.

Acknowledge that each child is unique and parents must be sensitive to the differences. These basic strategies can be used effectively with all children.

❺ Planning Your Personal Strategy

Objective:
To enable parents to identify the strategies they need to add to their tool box of parenting skills (5-10 minutes).

Ask parents to quickly review the list of strategies. Have them circle the numbers of two or three ideas that they want to personally develop.

Conclude by referring back to the initial Scripture passage from Luke 14:25-34 in terms of helping the parents retain their "saltiness." If the group is small enough for everyone to pray, keep the whole group together. Otherwise, divide into smaller groups.

Either in one large group or a few smaller groups, have everyone stand in a circle, holding hands. Invite the parents to pray this statement: **The parenting strategy that might help me keep my saltiness is _____ . Lord, help me to know how to do this.** Encourage them to fill in the strategy they'd like to make more a part of their parenting toolbox.

Where Do We Go from Here?
13

Session Aim:

To provide parents practical suggestions for helping their children avoid violence and become street smart and to encourage them to be catalysts for developing a healthier community.

Thirteen weeks have passed. Look out the window. It's the same world. Violence is still all around us. The media still assaults our senses with all kinds of messages. Many of those messages aren't very nice. Our kids are still tempted by all kinds of things. We haven't escaped family pressures.

Over the past thirteen weeks a lot of information has been shared. Where do we go from here? Some will walk away with some bits and pieces of information that will make them better parents. Others will ignore the very principles that could really help them. They'll keep doing the same old things. A few individuals may be fired up for making a big change. The study has given them some tools needed to make a difference in the lives of their children. Hooray!

In our violent world, our kids need to know where to go and where not to go.

Getting Ready:

Scriptures:
Romans 12:9-21.

1. Provide large poster boards or newsprint for the map exercise in Step 1. You will need one board for each team of three people.
2. Provide enough marking pens so that each team of three people can have a black marker, plus a red, blue, and green marking pen (substitute other colors if necessary).
3. If the kids of the parents in your group are highly mobile (beyond a defined neighborhood), obtain several copies of a regional map of your area.
4. Make four posters to place around the room:
   COMMUNITY INVOLVEMENT
   FAMILY
   SCHOOL
   PEER ENVIRONMENT
5. Photocopy "Street Smarts for Kids" (RS-13A), "Gang Information Sheet" (RS-13B), and " 'Deliver Us from Evil' " (RS-13C) for everyone.
6. For the optional activity at the end of Step 2, arrange for a local police officer to address the group for fifteen minutes.
7. If possible, provide a cassette recorder and tape to play some soft instrumental music during the reflection time in Step 4.

❶ Preparing for the Future

Objective:
To identify places in the community that children should avoid, go to for help, and become involved in positive activities (15 minutes).

As you begin this session, divide the group into teams of three and provide each team with a poster board, a black marker, and three different colored markers (e.g., red, blue, and green).

In our violent world, our kids need to know where to go and where not to go. They need to know what to do if they are faced with violence or the threat of it. In this activity, we'll try and provide some guidelines.

In small groups of three, have the participants draw maps of your neighborhood. They don't have to be to scale or very pretty, but they should have a few of the basic landmarks: major streets, parks, notable buildings, stores, etc.

On their maps, instruct the parents to indicate with a red marker places of potential violence. This could mean homes where parents allow children to do anything they want, areas with a high-crime profile, loitering sites for gangbangers, or drug houses.

Indicate with a blue marker places the children could go

A lack of knowledge in a violent culture could lead to serious injury, even death.

for help. Identify the fire stations, police stations, and youth centers they should know about.

Indicate with a green marker places where the children could get involved with positive activities. These might include: a church with a good youth program, parachurch organizations, drop-in centers, Y's, supervised gyms, Little League, soccer programs, homes of families with shared values, etc.

Have the teams share their maps with the whole group.

Encourage parents to repeat this exercise with their children, providing a chance to talk with their children about why some places are safe while others are not. The children might know of dangerous places and positive resources that their parents are not aware of.

Option: If the kids of the parents in your group are highly mobile (beyond a defined neighborhood), distribute copies of a regional map of your area to each small group. Using the designated colored markers, have the parents put numbers on the maps to identify places of violence, help, and positive activities, as described above. Then on an accompanying sheet of newsprint, have them duplicate the colored numbers listing the corresponding locations. For instance, "fire station" might be written next to the blue number 2, "supervised gym" next to the green number 4, etc.

❷ Not Getting Overwhelmed by Fear

Objective:
To identify street-smart wisdom that our children need to possess (10-20 minutes).

Do we want to teach our children to fear the world they live in? No. However, they need to respect what is happening in the world and understand the consequences. Children should have a healthy understanding of the world they live in and not be uninformed or naive. A lack of knowledge in a violent culture could lead to serious injury, even death. They should be able to pick up clues or signals that indicate possible dangerous situations. It is good to be able to think safely and heed warnings. Youth need to be equipped with decision-making skills to stay out of trouble.

Distribute copies of "Street Smarts for Kids" (RS-13A) and allow a few minutes for the parents to identify the areas where their children might need a "few more smarts."

Also pass out copies of "Gang Information Sheet" (RS-13B). It will be particularly helpful for parents of older children.

***O**ur kids need to be street smart and know what to look for and what to do if they see trouble coming their way.*

However, it contains information that every parent should know.

If you have time, discuss the prevalence of gang activity in your community according to the trends and definitions on the resource sheet. If you do not have time, go on to the next point.

Our kids need to be street smart and know what to look for and what to do if they see trouble coming their way. Remember the exercise in Session 5 when we drew pictures of a culturally relevant, media-oriented child? Let's do the same thing. But this time draw a picture of the street-smart kid. What does he or she need to have in order to make it in the world? (Possibly big eyes, in order to clearly see what is happening in the particular surroundings. Quick feet in order to run, if they see trouble coming their way. A razor-sharp mind for making quick decisions. Open, nonthreatening hands, and a closed mouth.)

This time do the exercise in the large group. Ask someone who is a good artist to draw the picture on the board. Use the drawing as a catalyst for talking about street smarts. Ask: **Are street smarts the same as common sense?** (Unfortunately, common sense doesn't take you as far as you need to go in uncommon situations.)

Draw out of the group what they feel are essential "street smarts" needed for your particular community.

Optional: Have a local police officer address the group for fifteen minutes (if you have time) about gang activity or other violence in your area and how to deal with it.

❸ Steps toward a Healthier Community

Objective:
To get input from the group regarding the health of their community and their recommendations for action the church could take (10 minutes).

Read the following to the group:
Search Institute of Minneapolis and Lutheran Brotherhood have published an evaluation guide to help people determine whether or not their community is a healthy place for youth. The guide is called, *Working Together for Youth.* **The researchers found four characteristics that distinguish healthy communities from less healthy ones. They are:**[1]

COMMUNITY INVOLVEMENT. This is described as a community where most youth are involved in some kind of structured activity within a religious,

In a healthy community, kids are tied into their families.

school, recreational, or community organization. Kids involved in these kinds of activities reported that they were building significant relationships with other adults in addition to their parents.

FAMILY. In a healthy community, kids are tied into their families. Parents love their kids, monitor their activities, discipline them, and are concerned about negative behaviors.

SCHOOL. In a healthy community, school is important. Kids care about school and attempt to do well. Parents are involved with their children through school activities.

PEER ENVIRONMENT. In a healthy community, young people have peers who are involved in positive activities and who don't buy into self-serving values. The kids in this kind of community don't skip school very much, and drinking parties are at a minimum.

Post the four charts around the room. One should have the heading COMMUNITY INVOLVEMENT, another FAMILY, another SCHOOL, another PEER ENVIRONMENT.

Have people gather under the chart that most interests them. They have two tasks:

1. Agree on a grade for their community: A, B, C, D, F.
2. Offer at least one quality suggestion for a way the church can help improve the quality of life in that area.

It's important to point out to the participants that our desire is to build up our community. That is a positive step toward making our communities violence free. That should be our goal. If we are unwilling to be catalysts for change, we will reap the consequences of our inactivity.

❹ Scriptural Encouragement

Objective:
To conclude this series with a sense of what God is calling us to be and do (10-15 minutes).

Romans 12:9-21 gives us some helpful insights into how we might respond to the culture of violence. Have everyone read Romans 12:9-21 silently. With soft music playing in the background, encourage the parents to reflect on the passage, asking the Lord to minister to them.

After they have finished, pass out " 'Deliver Us from Evil' " (RS-13C), and ask everyone to stand in a circle. As a responsive reading, have the parents read the bold-faced lines while you respond with the lines in normal print.

Sing "Amazing Grace" together, and close by reciting the Lord's Prayer together.

If your group would not be comfortable with singing, simply close in prayer asking God's blessing on all the children and parents or with the Lord's Prayer.

Notes:

1. I. Shelby Andress, *Working Together for Youth* (Minneapolis: Lutheran Brotherhood), 1993.

Bibliography

Basic Parenting Resources

Arp, Dave and Claudia. *PEP Groups for PARENTS of TEENS: Building Positive Relationships for the Teen Years*. Elgin, Ill.: David C. Cook Publishing Co., 1994.

Canfield, Ken R. *The Seven Secrets of Effective Fathers*. Wheaton, Ill.: Tyndale House, 1992.

Covey, Stephen R. *The Seven Habits of Highly Effective People: Restoring the Character Ethic*. New York: Simon and Schuster, 1989.

Curran, Delores. *Traits of a Healthy Family*. San Francisco: Harper and Row, 1983.

Dobson, James. *Love Must Be Tough*. Waco, Tex.: Word Books, 1983.

_____. *Parenting Isn't for Cowards*. Waco, Tex.: Word Books, 1987.

Elkind, David. *All Grown Up and No Place to Go: Teenagers in Crisis*. Reading Mass.: Addison-Wesley Publishing Co., 1984.

Eyre, Linda and Richard. *Teaching Your Children Values*. New York: Simon and Schuster, 1993.

Faber, Adele and Mazlish, Elaine. *How to Talk So Kids Will Listen and Listen So Kids Will Talk*. New York: Avon Books, 1980.

Glenn, H. Stephen and Nelsen, Jane. *Raising Self-Reliant Children in a Self-Indulgent World*. Rocklin, Calif.: Prima Publishing and Communications, 1989.

Huggins, Kevin. *Parenting Adolescents*. Colorado Springs, Colo.: NavPress, 1989.

Korem, Dan. *Streetwise Parents—Foolproof Kids*. Colorado Springs, Colo.: NavPress, 1992.

Leman, Kevin. *Bringing Up Kids Without Tearing Them Down*. New York: Delacorte Press, 1993.

_____. *Keeping Your Family Together When the World Is Falling Apart*. New York: Delacorte Press, 1992.

Schiller, Barbara. *Just Me & the Kids: Building Healthy Single-Parent Families*. Elgin, Ill.: David C. Cook Publishing Co., 1994.

Swindoll, Charles R. *The Strong Family*. Portland Ore.: Multnomah Press, 1991.

Warren, Ramona. *Parenting Alone, Studies for Single Parents*. Elgin, Ill.: David C. Cook Publishing Co., 1993.

Discipline

Arterburn, Stephen and Burns, Jim. *When Love Is Not Enough: Parenting through Tough Times*. Colorado Springs, Colo.: Focus on the Family Publishing, 1992.

Chase, Betty N. *Discipline Them, Love Them*. Elgin, Ill.: David C. Cook Publishing Co., 1982.

Glenn, H. Stephen; Lott, Lynn; and Nelsen, Jane. *Positive Discipline A-Z*. Rocklin, Calif.: Prima Publishing and Communications, 1993.

Nelsen, Jane. *Positive Discipline*. New York: Ballantine, 1987.

Nelsen, Jane and Lott, Lynn. *I'm On Your Side: Resolving Conflict with Your Teenage Son or Daughter*. Rocklin, Calif.: Prima Publishing and Communications, 1990.

Troubled Kids and Violence

Benson, Peter L. *The Troubled Journey*. Minneapolis, Minn.: Search Institute, 1993.

Dobson, James. *Love Must Be Tough*. Waco, Tex.: Word Books, 1983.

Garbarino, James. *Let's Talk about Living in a World with Violence, an Activity Book for School-Age Children*. Chicago: Erikson Institute, 1993.

McLean, Gordon. *Danger at Your Door*. Westchester, Ill: Crossway Books, 1984.

McLean, Gordon with Jackson, Dave and Neta. *Cities of Lonesome Fear: God Among the Gangs*. Chicago: Moody Press, 1991.

Oliver, Gary Jackson and Wright, H. Norman. *When Anger Hits Home*. Chicago: Moody Press, 1992.

Cultural Issues

Bennett, William J. *The Index of Leading Cultural Indicators*. New York: Simon and Schuster, 1994.

Blythe, Dale A. with Roehlkepartain, Eugene C. *Healthy Communities, Healthy Youth*. Minneapolis, Minn.: Search Institute, 1993.

DeMoss, Robert G. *Learn to Discern*. Grand Rapids, Mich.: Zondervan Publishing House, 1992.

Dobson, James and Bauer, Gary. *Children at Risk: The Battle for the Hearts and Minds of Our Kids*. Dallas, Tex.: Word Publishing, 1990.

Family Research Council. *Free to Be Family: Helping Mothers and Fathers Meet the Needs of the Next Generation of American Children*. Washington, D.C.: Family Research Council, 1992.

Kilpatrick, William. *Why Johnny Can't Tell Right from Wrong: Moral Literacy and the Case for Character Education*. New York: Simon and Schuster, 1992.

Medved, Michael. *Hollywood vs. America: Popular Culture and the War on Traditional Values*. San Francisco: Harper Collins and Grand Rapids, Mich.: Zondervan, 1992.

Schultze, Quentin J. *Dancing in the Dark: Youth, Popular Culture, and the Electronic Media*. Grand Rapids, Mich.: W.B. Eerdmans Pub. Co., 1991.

Memory Ticklers

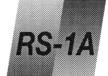

Cut apart the following "memory ticklers" and place them in a hat or basket so each person can draw one and respond.

Describe your best friend.	What did your parents do to aggravate you?	State your biggest question about life.	Describe a typical summer day.
Recall a church memory.	What did you want to be when you grew up?	What could friends do to aggravate you?	Recall what you did on weekends.
Tell of a frightening time.	Describe an adult who made an impact on your life.	What was a major decision you had to make?	What were your dreams?
What made you laugh?	What was a common slang expression?	Name a favorite song in high school.	Describe your favorite teacher.
Tell of a silly stunt you did.	Name a favorite musical group.	Describe your favorite hangout.	In what school activity were you most involved?
What did you do to aggravate your parents?	What was your biggest worry?	What was your favorite TV program?	Describe a favorite family memory.

Violence: Then and Now

For each of the categories listed in the left column below, jot down memories of violence from your youth and thoughts about violence today.

	Then	Now
Television		
Movies		
Music		
Local news		
National news		
Society's reaction		
The cause (Who's to blame?)		

Too Much Violence

RS-1C

For each type of violence, check all the categories that apply. If it has happened more than once, put the actual number in the appropriate box.

	It happened to me	I saw it happen to someone	It happened to someone in my family	It happened to a close friend	It happened to someone I know	I'm afraid it will happen to me
1. A fight where someone was hurt						
2. A knife fight						
3. A shooting						
4. Wounded by a bullet						
5. Killed						
6. Raped						
7. Date-raped						
8. Robbed						
9. Shaken down for money						
10. Bike or other valuable stolen						
11. Attacked by a gang of three or more						
12. Stalked on the street						
13. Received threatening notes or calls						
14. Warned to stay away from certain places						
15. A valuable possession vandalized						
16. Carried a gun to school						
17. Carried some other weapon to school						
18. Seriously considered suicide						
19. Committed suicide						
20. Observed a drug deal						

Survey Result Questions

Discuss the following questions based on the survey from last week.

- **What was the reaction of your child(ren) to answering questions about violence?**

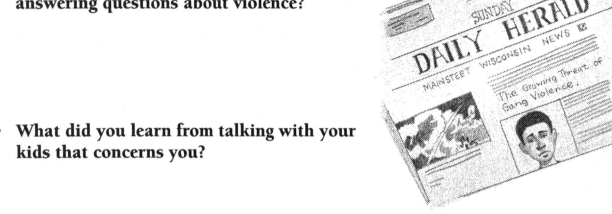

- **What did you learn from talking with your kids that concerns you?**

- **Did you learn anything from the discussion with your child(ren) that made you feel more at ease?**

- **How did their answers differ from what you expected?**

- **Are your children's perceptions about violence different from those you hold? How does that make you feel?**

Listen to the Children

The following quotations came from grade-school-age children in Chicago who entered a writing contest called, "My Neighborhood." It was an appeal to younger residents to show civic pride. What came back shocked the adults who sponsored the contest.*

Go around the small group and take turns reading the children's reports.

Six year old: "The houses in my neighborhood look so pretty, but I don't see my neighborhood much. . . . I only go outside when I get in the car or go to school. I don't like my neighborhood because they shoot too much. They might shoot me. So, I stay in the house. . . . One time, some bullets hit our window. I was afraid. My house doesn't seem safe anymore. Maybe, I should hide under my bed. Then I won't get shot. My dog is missing. . . . Maybe they shot him. Maybe they shot him so they can rob my house. My neighborhood is getting worse. . . . Maybe, everyone should just move."

A second grader drew a large home with purple windows and a bright-faced boy in the door. But at the top of the poster board he wrote: "My neighborhood is bad . . . you will die."

Ten year old: "People get killed by shooting mostly every night."

Fifth grader: "My neighborhood is like being in jail. [I'm] scared to go outside because you were threatened that you were going to get beat up. And if you tell anybody you and the person you tell going to get shot."

Second grade girl: "One day I saw three dead bodies being pulled out of the building."

Thirteen year old: "I don't want to be one lesser black male dead. . . . My neighborhood is so bad that if you gave any fool a gun with no bullets he would try his best to shoot it. As you might know I live in a slum. Some people call it hell on earth and so do I."

Eleven year old: "These are the things in my neighborhood I see. It doesn't seem like I'm free. We cry, we weep, we can't go outside and play because our parents believe we will be killed that day."

In many of the entries the only hope expressed was in the hereafter. After giving an elaborate description of the gang killing in his neighborhood, one **third grader** wrote, "Only God can heal us."

What are these children and our children trying to teach us about growing up in a violent society? Are their concerns similar or different from your children?

Parents Look at Violence

RS-2C

Fill out the following questionnaire. Check all that apply.

1. *My definition of violence:*

2. *The evidence of violence most prevalent in our community is:*

3. *As a result of living in a more violent culture I . . .*

    __ *am angry.*
    __ *tolerate more.*
    __ *feel less in control.*
    __ *feel helpless.*
    __ *feel like I need more help in coping.*
    __ *feel as if my child is being impacted negatively*
       by all the changes that are taking place.
    __ *am more afraid.*
    __ *want to move to a safer place.*
    __ *want to equip my child to deal with*
       all the struggles that are coming.
    __ *find myself needing to be equipped.*

4. *The kinds of violence I am concerned about for my kids are . . .*

    __ *physical assaults.*
    __ *verbal assaults.*
    __ *date rape.*
    __ *shootings.*
    __ *ordinary fighting.*
    __ *kidnapping.*
    __ *gang-related activities.*
    __ *what they see on TV.*
    __ *what they see in print.*
    __ *what they hear on the radio.*
    __ *what they hear in popular music.*
    __ *random violence.*
    __ *muggings.*

Cultural Messages

CULTURAL MESSAGE	HOW IS IT BEING SPREAD?	HOW AM I AFFECTED?	SPIRITUAL RESPONSES
1. Materialism: The most important thing in life is the ownership of possessions.			**Matthew 19:21-25**
2. Existentialism: Live for the moment; it's all that you have.			**Hebrews 4:12, 13**
3. Individualism: The most important person in your life is you.			**Matthew 22:37-40**
4. Hedonism: Pleasure, happiness, and fun are the primary purposes of life.			**Romans 12:2**
5. Secularism: God is not significant. At best He is irrelevant.			**Exodus 20:1-3**
6. Naturalism: Human life has no more value than an owl or a tree.			**Psalm 8:3-8**
7. Utopianism: Humans are basically good. Just give them a good environment and all evil will vanish.			**Romans 3:9-18**
8. Anti-historicism: Truth is relative and not as important as being politically correct.			**John 15:26**
9. Pragmatism: If it works do it.			**Psalm 119:1-4**
10. Moral relativism: No absolutes. There are no rights, no wrongs.			**Deuteronomy 26:16-19**
11. Victimism: I am the way I am because of what other people have done to me.			**Matthew 19:26**

Violent Acts

How might the person(s) involved justify his or her actions based on cultural messages?

1. A group of teenage girls meet at a friend's house and try to convince her to get an abortion to eliminate her unwanted pregnancy.

2. It is Halloween. Your child is out with some friends. The group decides to start fires in abandoned buildings.

3. The Sisters, a girls' gang, attend a house party. A rival gang drives by and call them all kinds of names. The Sisters take off after them to get revenge.

4. As the head of a major corporation, you are facing an economic slump. An opportunity presents itself to buy ad time on a television show that degrades the family. The television show is top rated and its audience profile matches the customer profile you most want to reach.

5. Your child is in a fight with a neighborhood friend. You watch and start yelling instructions to your child.

6. Your child wants to buy a video game you know is very violent. Her reason for wanting the game is that everyone else has one. You say okay because you don't want to deprive her.

7. Your neighbor hits both his spouse and children regularly. You choose to look the other way.

8. You teach your child how to get in a good lick in the middle of a football pile-up.

9. Your old boyfriend who dropped you for no apparent reason, walks down the hall with a girl you can't stand. You make plans to retaliate.

10. A family of another racial background moves into your neighborhood. You talk to your husband about selling your home and moving out of the neighborhood.

11. On a date, you get turned on physically and despite your partner's protests you force her into having sex with you.

12. You are a doctor pledged to help people live life fully. One of your older patients is terminally ill and in tremendous pain. He doesn't want to live any longer and asks you to help deliver him from the pain through an assisted suicide.

13. Your family has owned property in the inner city for years. Some might call you a slum lord. The buildings you own don't make a lot of money and would be very expensive to rehabilitate. While run down, they do provide basic shelter for people.

14. An actress has had several abortions. She pickets regularly in front of an upscale store that sells furs.

15. A movie producer wants to film a movie geared to younger audiences. The script calls for several nude scenes and dozens of acts of random violence which are designed to help box office receipts.

16. Your mother and grandmother have quick tempers. You often lose your temper with other people and let them know exactly how you feel. When asked why, you say, "I can't help it."

17. A teenager sees a stranger with the athletic shoes he wants. He has spent his money on some other things but wants these shoes. He steals them from the stranger.

18. A group of young men decide to have a contest to see who can have sex with the most young women in a four-week time period.

19. When asked why she hurt another child, the four year old said, "They do it on television."

20. It is discovered that a known child molester was sexually abused as a child. News coverage indicates that his behavior is to be expected given his background.

What Our Kids Are Saying Today

Draw lines between the comments kids might say on the left and the corresponding cultural messages or "-isms" on the right.

KIDS' COMMENTS

1. "If my old man was rich, then I could make it."

2. "Yeah, I cheated. So what? I passed the test didn't I?"

3. "I blew it this time, but give me time. I'll get better."

4. "What's God ever done for me?"

5. "Everybody else has the latest video recorder and we've got this old one."

6. "What about me?"

7. "When you die, that's it, right?"

8. "Just because it's wrong for you, doesn't mean it's wrong for me."

9. "I'm going to enjoy myself as much as possible now. Tomorrow may never come."

10. "Party hearty! Have a good time."

11. "All politicians lie, so what?"

CULTURAL MESSAGES

a. Materialism:
   The most important thing in life is the ownership of possessions.

b. Existentialism:
   Live for the moment; it's all that you have.

c. Individualism:
   The most important person in your life is you.

d. Hedonism:
   Pleasure, happiness, and fun are the primary purposes of life.

e. Secularism:
   God is not significant. At best He is irrelevant.

f. Naturalism:
   Human life has no more value than an owl or a tree.

h. Utopianism:
   Humans are basically good. Just start give them a good environment, and all evil will vanish.

i. Anti-historicism:
   Truth isn't as important as being politically correct.

j. Pragmatism:
   If it works do it.

k. Moral relativism:
   No absolutes. There are no rights, no wrongs.

l. Victimism:
   I can't make my own choices because of what other people have done to me.

Write a comment that you think your child might make that reflects one of the above messages.

The Whole Armor of God

✔ = *That's me!*
0 = *Not me yet.*

Truth

__ The Bible is my primary source for truth.

__ I am able to discern truth from false teachings.

Righteousness

__ I am confident that I am in right standing with God because I have put my trust in Christ.

__ I may not be perfect, but holy living is my daily goal.

Peace

__ In my last crisis, I responded calmly.

__ I usually don't worry about things.

Faith

__ Although a lot of negative things have occurred to my family, I still believe God will work things out.

__ I look forward to the future.

Salvation

__ I know that Christ lives inside me.

__ The most important thing in my life is that my children become Christians.

Holy Spirit

__ I understand how to be controlled by the Holy Spirit.

__ I know how powerful the Holy Spirit is and what He can do in my life and in the lives of my children.

Bible

__ My strength and direction come from God's Word.

__ I read and explain the Bible to my children.

Prayer

__ I have established a regular devotional time.

__ I pray for my family daily.

Look at the zeros on the page. Are there holes in your armor? Your group leader has some repair suggestions.

Kids and the Media

Here are several quotes about how our culture impacts our children.

1. "Those who defend contemporary rap music, with its extravagantly brutal and obscene lyrics, do not generally condone the conduct described in the songs; they suggest, rather, that it is inappropriate to judge such material on a moral basis. By the same token, producers of movies or TV shows that seem to glorify violent or promiscuous behavior do not insist that watching these entertainments is actually good for you. Instead, they maintain that the images they create amount to a "value-neutral" experience, with no real impact on the viewer and no underlying influence on society. The apologists for the entertainment industry seldom claim that Hollywood's messages are beneficial; they argue, rather that those messages don't matter."
   —Film critic Michael Medved in *Hollywood vs. America* (San Francisco: Harper Collins and Grand Rapids, Mich.: Zondervan, 1992), 23.

2. "Violence without consequence is a theme of our times. A young person told a counselor he couldn't believe he felt pain after being shot. All the shootings he had ever watched on television were of painless death or injuries."
   —*Implications*, Fall, 1992.

3. "The more hours of television children and adults watch, we've found the more pessimistic and deterministic they are in life—and the more they look at themselves and say, 'Since I'm not big and powerful, why bother—I have no control. Since I don't have those assets, I don't matter.' We've raised a generation of young people who, rather than being involved in meaningful things, in families, in institutions, spend more of their childhood watching the media—a media that overwhelms them, defeats them and gives them invalid role models."
   — "The Second Birth Called Adolescence, a Conversation with Stephen Glenn," *Youth Worker Update*, Winter/1994, 60-61.

Continued

4. "When criticized about the content of TV shows, television executives are quick to point out that their programs merely reflect American life. Their standard retort: 'The problem is in society, not with the media.' To test the claim that TV does not mold but only mimics American life, researchers watched a week of prime-time TV . . . and concluded that any resemblance between the values and behaviors of TV characters and any actual person, living or dead, is purely coincidental."
—*Youth Worker Update*, September 1993, 4.

5. "Violent messages in the media are aimed with particular intensity at the very young and have become a major feature of so-called children's programming."
—Film critic Michael Medved in *Hollywood vs. America* (San Francisco: Harper Collins and Grand Rapids, Mich.: Zondervan, 1992), 247.

6. "By graduation day, the average high school student has seen 18,000 murders in 22,000 hours of television viewing. According to studies done at the Annenburg School of Communication in Philadelphia, 55 percent of prime-time characters are involved in violent confrontations once a week. . . . Dr. Leonard D. Efrom, Professor of Psychology at the University of Illinois at Chicago, conducted a 22 year study of 400 TV viewers. He concluded, 'There can no longer be any doubt that heavy exposure to televised violence is one of the causes of aggressive behavior, crime and violence in our society.'"
—James Dobson and Gary L. Bauer, *Children at Risk* (Word Books 1990), 206, 207.

7. "According to Nielsen Media Research, teenagers ages 12-17 watch TV an average of 22 hours a week. And according to educational consultant Jawanza Kunjufu, many urban Black children watch more than twice that much. That's more hours than are spent at school and doing homework combined. We must be careful not to allow profit-driven advertisers to turn our kids into mindless junkies who will do anything for a pair of sneakers so 'I can be like Mike.'"
—Spencer Perkins, "Confronting Today's Crisis in Youth Values," *Urban Family* magazine, Winter, 1992, 19-20.

Continued

8. "Because I know words matter, I wish my children, and kids younger than my children, would get back to innocent, hopeful lyrics. I wish their music was more about love and less graphically about intercourse. I wish their songs could be less angry and 'victimized' and more about building a better world. I wish their songs could be more like ours."
   —William Raspberry, *Washington Post*, September 18, 1993. As reported in *Youth Worker Update*, November 1993.

9. "We're raising a generation of youngsters who are numb to violence and hatred, who know death at close hand and who seriously doubt, as children never should, that they will survive to reach adulthood and middle age. Joblessness, hopelessness, miseducation, family deterioration, erosion of fundamental values—all these things contribute to our children's loss of innocence."
   —William Raspberry, *Washington Post*, July 8, 1993. As reported in *Youth Worker Update*, September 1993.

10. "In my capacity as the youth culture specialist for Focus on the Family, I and my staff transcribed [the lyrics from a] double record set and found . . .
   87 descriptions of oral sex
   117 explicit references to male and female genitalia
   226 uses of the F___ word
   163 uses of bitch when referring to women
   81 uses of the vulgarity sh__
   42 uses of ass
Among this garbage heap of lyrical imagery, the band added a reference to incest, several instances of group sex, and over a dozen illustrations of violent sexual acts. . . .
   "When it comes to the question of music's influence upon the listener, a bit of common sense is in order. We must avoid making two equally disastrous mistakes: (1) blaming all of a child's problems upon the impact of his music, and (2) dismissing any possible relationship between what a child listens to and what a child does."
   —Robert G. DeMoss, *Learn to Discern* (Grand Rapids, Mich.: Zondervan 1992), 68, 81.

Continued

11. " 'Parent's Music Resource Center's Rock Music Report' in 1985 concludes that 'the average teenager listens to rock music an average of 4 to 6 hours daily,' and that 'from grades seven through twelve the average teen listens (in six years) to 190,650 hours of music; compared to 11,000 hours listening to a teacher.' "
—*Implications* magazine, Summer 1991, Vol. 4, Issue 1, p. 2.

12. "Here's how I perceive how the electronic media has affected the kids in your youth group and set them apart from kids of twenty years ago.
- Kids in your groups are more alike.... They think alike, talk alike, dress alike, know the same stories, idolize the same celebrities, eat the same fast food, have the same values....
- Kids in your group are more passive.... Thanks to the modern media, your students have learned that there is no necessary relationship between information and action.
- Kids in your group are less creative.... Kids who grow up with television are not used to creating their own stories, their own play, their own entertainment. They expect technology to amuse them.
- Kids in your group are busier.... 'Television,' writes Richard Louv in *Childhood's Future*, 'is a thief of time....'
- Kids in your group are more jaded.... They've seen it all. Nothing shocks them.... Overexposure to violence, rough language, sexual situation, murder, and death has numbed kids....
- Kids in your group think differently.... television has created a world of watchers who require fast action, quick cuts, special effects, and sound bytes to hold their attention."
—Wayne Rice, "A Word from the Editor," *Youth Worker Update*, Fall, 1991.

Hollywood vs. God's Commandments

✂ —

God says, "You shall have no other gods before me" (Exod. 20:3), and "Worship the Lord your God, and serve him only" (Matt. 4:10).

✂ —

God says, "You shall not make for yourself an idol" (Exod. 20:4), and "No servant can serve two masters" (Luke 16:13).

✂ —

God says, "You shall not misuse the name of the Lord your God" (Exod. 20:7), and "Do not swear at all" (Matt. 5:34).

✂ —

God says, "Remember the Sabbath day by keeping it holy" (Exod. 20:8).

✂ —

God says, "Honor your father and your mother" (Exod. 20:12).

✂ —

God says, "You shall not murder" (Exod. 20:13), and "Anyone who is angry with his brother will be subject to judgment" (Matt. 5:22).

✂ —

God says, "You shall not commit adultery" (Exod. 20:14), and "Anyone who looks at a woman lustfully has already committed adultery with her in his heart" (Matt. 5:28).

✂ —

God says, "You shall not steal" (Exod. 20:15).

✂ —

God says, "You shall not give false testimony" (Exod. 20:16), and "Men will have to give account on the day of judgment for every careless word they have spoken" (Matt. 12:36).

✂ —

God says, "You shall not covet" (Exod. 20:17), and "Be on your guard against all kinds of greed" (Luke 12:15).

✂ —

Media Helps for Our Home

- Make all television viewing intentional. Review the television guide each week and choose the programs you will watch ahead of time.
- Watch all television programs with your child so you can turn off anything that is morally or spiritually offensive.
- For preschoolers, do not use television or a video as a baby-sitter.
- Set a maximum weekly viewing time for each child based on age. This time may not be "banked" or carried over to next week.
- Examine your own media intake. Are you digesting ungodly material and modeling inappropriate viewing or listening habits to your kids?
- Model for your kids activities such as reading and hobbies— active things that don't allow them to be passive.
- Keep a bookshelf of good Christian books and classics in the same room as the television. Read with your children often.
- Agree on family standards for video viewing. Only G or G and PG ratings, etc. Maintain "veto power" over any videos brought into the home.
- Talk with your children about things they watch and listen to. Ask questions like:
  — What are you watching (or listening to)?
  — What is this program or tape's message?
  — Is this program or video trying to persuade you to act a certain way? If so, what?
  — How does this fit with your faith?
  — Is it asking you to do anything that Jesus wouldn't approve of?

Dialog is a means of helping kids "learn to discern" which should be a goal of ours.

- Explain your reasons for your standards, and involve your older kids in the decision-making process.
- Be consistent in your standards.
- Introduce your kids to Christian and healthy secular alternatives.

A Media Plan of Action for My Family

Media issues I need to be alert for:

Media messages I'm afraid might be coming into our home:

Media messages my kids are getting that concern me:

What part of a new media policy in our home do I need to discuss with my children?

Who Am I?*

Read through the following statements and indicate your degree of agreement or disagreement with an "X" on the scale to the right.

1. Adolescents have a need to find out who they are: how they are different from their family; how they feel about things; what their own values are; and what they think about things. This process is called *individuation*.

2. Individuation usually looks like rebellion to parents. Although most parents worry when their teens rebel, it would be more appropriate to worry if they didn't. At first, individuation is primarily a reaction against their parents.

3. Parents would prefer to have their kids mature slowly, but nature has its own patterns. The physical, emotional, sexual, and biological processes produce contradictory feelings in kids.

4. The physical maturation process, with its sudden and powerful hormonal changes, causes mood swings.

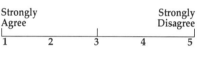

5. Teens need to work out their relationships with peers to find out if and how they fit in.

6. Teens have a strong desire to find out what they're capable of—they need to test their power and importance in the world. This means that they want to decide what they can do for themselves without being directed and ordered. However, some teens find this so intimidating that they want others, usually their peers, to tell them what to do.

7. Teens have a great need for privacy so they can work out a lot of the already mentioned tasks without an audience.

8. During this period, teens tend to put their parents down and try to show them how "stupid" they are.

9. Teens think of themselves as omnipotent and all-knowing.

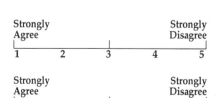

* Adapted from Jane Nelsen and Lynn Lott, *I'm On Your Side* (Rocklin, Calif.: Prima Publishing and Communication, 1990).

External Assets

Study each of the following assets and suggest one or more ideas for how you as a parent can encourage this asset in your child.

*Factors That Surround Youth to Help Them Grow Up Healthy**

1. Family support—Family life provides high levels of love and support.

2. Parents as social resources—Youth turn to parents for advice and support.

3. Parent communication—Youth have frequent, in-depth conversations with parents.

4. Other adult resources—Youth turn to nonparent adults for advice and support.

5. Other adult communication—Youth often have in-depth conversations with other adults.

6. Parent involvement in school—Parents are involved in helping youth succeed in school.

7. Positive school climate—School provides a caring, encouraging environment.

8. Parental standards—Parents have standards for appropriate conduct.

9. Parental discipline—Parents discipline youth when rules are violated.

10. Parental monitoring—Parents monitor youth's whereabouts.

11. Time at home—Youth spend time at home at least four nights a week.

12. Positive peer influence—Youth's best friends model responsible behavior.

13. Music—Youth spend time in music training or practice.

14. Extracurricular activities—Youth are involved in school sports, clubs, or organizations.

15. Community activities—Youth are involved in organizations or clubs outside school.

16. Church involvement—Youth regularly attend religious programs or services.

Place a star in front of the three strongest external assets of your children.
Circle three assets that need to be developed in your children.

* "Ideas for Building External Assets in Youth," *Youth Update*, August 1993, pp. 4, 5. Used by permission of Search Institute.

Internal Assets

Study each of the following assets and suggest one or more ideas for how you as a parent can encourage this asset in your child.

Commitments, Values, and Skills That Help Youth Make Healthy Choices*

1. **Achievement motivation**—Youth are motivated to achieve in school.	
2. **Educational aspiration**—Youth aspire to post-high school education.	
3. **School performance**—Youth do well in school.	
4. **Homework**—Youth regularly spend time doing homework.	
5. **Values helping people**—Youth believe it is important to help other people.	
6. **Global concern**—Youth are concerned about world issues such as world hunger.	
7. **Empathy**—Youth care about other people's feelings.	
8. **Values sexual restraint**—Youth believe it is important to abstain from sex before marriage.	
9. **Assertiveness skills**—Youth are assertive in standing up for what they believe.	
10. **Decision-making skills**—Youth are good at making decisions.	
11. **Friendship-making skills**—Youth are good at making friends.	
12. **Planning skills**—Youth know how to plan ahead.	
13. **Self-esteem**—Youth have a high self-esteem.	
14. **Hope**—Youth have a positive view of their personal future.	

* "Ideas for Building Internal Assets in Youth," *Youth Update*, November 1993, pp. 4, 5. Used by permission of Search Institute.

Signs of Trouble!
There's a Storm Brewing

Check off the at-risk behaviors that Joey exhibits.

- ☐ Becomes friends with kids you've never heard of
- ☐ Begins to exhibit a negative personality change
- ☐ Behaves in an excessively selfish manner
- ☐ Carelessly violates curfew but with "good" excuses
- ☐ Carries a weapon
- ☐ Ceases to bring friends home
- ☐ Changes dress or appearance dramatically
- ☐ Chews tobacco frequently
- ☐ Criticizes straight kids
- ☐ Defends peers' right to use drugs
- ☐ Desires to drop out of school
- ☐ Displays pictures of gang symbols in room
- ☐ Drops out of sports or extracurricular activities
- ☐ Emotionally pulls away from family
- ☐ Engages in binge drinking
- ☐ Evades questions about where he goes and what he does
- ☐ Exhibits defensiveness about friends
- ☐ Experiences deep depression
- ☐ Experiences extreme weight loss or gain
- ☐ Explodes in violent behavior or speech
- ☐ Expresses hostility toward all police
- ☐ Expresses hostility toward adults or authority figures
- ☐ Expresses seductive, promiscuous behavior
- ☐ Gets a tattoo with a gang symbol

- ☐ Gets fired from a job
- ☐ Has unusual and or secretive phone calls
- ☐ Increases isolation
- ☐ Is dissatisfied with how much freedom is allowed
- ☐ Is expelled from school
- ☐ Is involved in group fights
- ☐ Is sexually active and does not use contraceptives
- ☐ Lies and searches for loopholes
- ☐ Misses school or is tardy without your knowledge
- ☐ Often uses hand signs with friends
- ☐ Possesses drug paraphernalia
- ☐ Receives grades much lower than usual
- ☐ Refuses to use seat belts
- ☐ Resists family values
- ☐ Runs away regularly
- ☐ Smokes
- ☐ Stays out all night
- ☐ Steals things
- ☐ Talks about considering suicide
- ☐ Uses a street name
- ☐ Uses alcohol frequently
- ☐ Valuables disappear from home
- ☐ Vandalizes things
- ☐ Wears clothing of a certain style and only certain colors

The Life of Absalom

Arrange the events of Absalom's life in the correct order. If you're not familiar with this story, skim: II Samuel 13:1, 8-14, 21-29, 37-39; 14:21-33; 15:1-10, 13, 14; 18:9-15, 33.

✂ — ✂ — — —

- Absalom's sister Tamar is raped by their stepbrother Amnon, one of David's son's.

✂ —

- David heard about the rape, and he was angry, but did nothing about it.

✂ —

- Absalom said nothing to Amnon after the rape of his sister, but two years later he had Amnon killed to avenge him for raping his sister.

✂ —

- Absalom fled after killing Amnon, and went to Geshur (where his mother's father and relatives lived), and David mourned for his son daily, but did nothing.

✂ —

- David sent for Absalom to return from Geshur to Jerusalem, but David took a long time to forgive Absalom and didn't want to see him. Absalom lived in Jerusalem for two years before David allowed him to come see him.

✂ —

- After seeing David, Absalom still rebelled and got several men to follow him. He revolted against his father and ran David out of the city and made himself king.

✂ —

- David's men pursued Absalom to restore David to the throne. They found Absalom hanging from a tree. He was then killed as he hung from the tree.

✂ —

- David wept bitterly and mourned the death of his son.

✂ —

Could My Child Turn Out Like Joey?

Complete a copy of this resource for each of your children. Read through the following statements and mark the strength of each asset in your child with an "X" on the scale to the right.

_____ **(Name of child)**

Has a vital, growing relationship with Jesus.

Weak _____ Strong

Has a home that is stable, secure, and loving.

Weak _____ Strong

Knows that he or she is capable.

Weak _____ Strong

Believes that he or she has unique gifts and talents to contribute.

Weak _____ Strong

Knows that he or she is not a victim but can influence what happens to him or her.

Weak _____ Strong

Is self-disciplined and knows how to be self-controlled. He or she knows how to select from a number of possible behaviors the appropriate response in a situation.

Weak _____ Strong

Knows how to assess his or her feelings and then act appropriately.

Weak _____ Strong

Knows how to cooperate with others.

Weak _____ Strong

Is responsible.

Weak _____ Strong

Listens to others.

Weak _____ Strong

Makes judgments based upon appropriate values.

Weak _____ Strong

Based on this look at my child, here is what I feel I can do to:

Nurture areas of strength _____

_____

Strengthen areas of weakness _____

_____

Solutions for the Picky Shopper

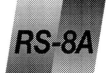

After hearing the report by Tony Evans about the boy who rejected every toy the clerk showed him, how would you complete the clerk's statement?

Cross out the responses that would not help the boy. Then rate the useful options by numbering them beginning with number one for the best solution, two for the next best, etc.

Folks, what this kid needs we don't sell here. He needs . . .

___ a new bike.

___ stylish, expensive clothes.

___ medication.

___ a concert experience.

___ a place to hang out.

___ to travel.

___ a therapist.

___ parents.

___ a good education.

___ friends.

___ something meaningful to do.

___ a job.

___ to be outside playing.

___ (your idea) _____

___ (your idea) _____

___ (your idea) _____

The Prodigal Son Improv

Select a different dramatic or artistic style to depict your assigned scene such as: western, melodrama, mystery, slapstick comedy, musical, soap opera, docudrama, rap, etc. Add narrators, investigative reporters, camera people, directors, or anyone else to the list of suggested characters.

SCENE 1, Luke 15:11-13

Characters: Father and younger son. The older son could be present. Party goers in the far land could be added.

Situation: The youngest son of a wealthy farmer requests his share of the estate now, instead of waiting until his father dies. His father is generous, and after expressing his concern about the wisdom of the son's choice, he divides his wealth between his two sons. A few days later the younger son packs all his belongings and travels to a distant land where he spends his money freely on parties and foolish living.

SCENE 2, Luke 15:14-19

Characters: Younger son, various people in the far land, and a pig farmer.

Situation: When the son's money is gone, a great famine sweeps over the land, and he begins to starve. Finally, he persuades a local farmer to hire him to feed his pigs. The boy becomes so hungry that even the pods he feeds the swine look good to him. He finally comes to his senses and realizes that even the hired men in his father's household have plenty of food to eat. He decides to return home and confess, "Father, I have sinned against both heaven and you, and am no longer worthy of being called your son. Please take me on as a hired man."

SCENE 3, Luke 15:20-24

Characters: Younger son, father, and servants.

Situation: The boy returns home. While he is still a long distance away, his father sees him coming, and runs to welcome him. The boy begins his pitch to become a servant, but the father orders the servants to prepare a feast. The father provides for the boy the finest robe in the house, a ring for his finger, and shoes. Once the celebration begins, the father says, "This son of mine was dead and has returned to life. He was lost and is found!"

SCENE 4, Luke 15:25-32

Characters: Younger son, father, servants, and older son.

Situation: When the older son returns from working in the fields, he hears music coming from the house and asks a servant what's going on. The servant tells him that his brother is back, his father has killed the fattened calf, and a great feast is prepared to celebrate the boy's return. The older brother is angry and will not go in. When the father comes out and begs him, the older son says, "All these years I've worked hard for you and never once refused to do a single thing you told me to. In all that time you never gave me even one young goat for a feast with my friends. Yet, when this son of yours comes back after spending your money on prostitutes, you celebrate by killing the finest calf we have on the place." The father explains that he and the older son have always been together and everything that was the father's belongs to the older son, but it is right to celebrate. "Your brother was as good as dead and has come back to life! He was lost and is found!"

Looking at the Strength of Our Family

STRENGTHS OF STRONG FAMILIES	HOW MY FAMILY MEASURES UP		WORTHY IDEAS
Our family is deeply committed to each other. The family is our highest priority next to our relationship with the Lord.	I SAY _____ WEAK STRONG	MY KIDS WOULD SAY _____ WEAK STRONG	
Our family is strongly committed to spending time together. We make it a point to frequently have quality time as a family unit. We frequently rearrange our schedules so we can spend time together.	I SAY _____ WEAK STRONG	MY KIDS WOULD SAY _____ WEAK STRONG	
Our family practices good communication. We make an effort to listen to each other and to focus on solutions. We spend one-on-one time with each other.	I SAY _____ WEAK STRONG	MY KIDS WOULD SAY _____ WEAK STRONG	
Our family shows appreciation for one another. We are able to joke and kid around at no one else's expense. We affirm each other, taking joy in each other's accomplishments.	I SAY _____ WEAK STRONG	MY KIDS WOULD SAY _____ WEAK STRONG	
Our family is committed to living our life together based on scriptural principles. We know the Lord is the foundation upon which we must build our family life.	I SAY _____ WEAK STRONG	MY KIDS WOULD SAY _____ WEAK STRONG	
Our family handles crises in a positive way. We see a crisis (large or small) as an opportunity to draw together instead of being drawn apart.	I SAY _____ WEAK STRONG	MY KIDS WOULD SAY _____ WEAK STRONG	

If I Sow . . . I Will Reap

If I sow seeds of love with my child, I might reap . . .

If I sow seeds of kindness with my child, I might reap . . .

If I sow seeds of patience with my child, I might reap . . .

If I sow seeds of envy with my child, I might reap . . .

If I sow seeds of pride with my child, I might reap . . .

If I sow seeds of rudeness with my child, I might reap . . .

If I sow seeds of selfishness with my child, I might reap . . .

If I sow seeds of anger with my child, I might reap . . .

If I sow seeds that delight in evil with my child, I might reap . . .

If I sow seeds of truthfulness with my child, I might reap . . .

If I sow seeds of protection with my child, I might reap . . .

If I sow seeds of hope with my child I might, reap . . .

If I sow seeds of perseverance with my child, I might reap . . .

Habits of Effective Christian Parents

STEPHEN COVEY'S PRINCIPLES*	APPLICATION FOR CHRISTIAN PARENTS	SCRIPTURAL PRINCIPLE
1. Be proactive. The action I take should be based upon self-chosen values instead of upon my moods, feelings, and circumstances.	An effective Christian parent makes choices based upon "faith principles" and scriptural insights. He or she doesn't have to base decisions on moods, circumstances, or feelings. Ineffective parents see themselves as victims of circumstance or other people. Effective parents know they have the ability to "choose" how they will respond. The ability to choose is a gift from God.	Deuteronomy 6:6, 7—"These commandments that I give you today are to be upon your hearts. Impress them on your children. Talk about them when you sit at home and when you walk along the road, when you lie down and when you get up."
2. Begin with the end in mind. I should know where I am going with my own life. Have I written a personal mission statement which provides meaning, purpose, and direction to my life? I need to make sure my actions focus on my mission.	God has a plan. Effective Christian parents prayerfully search for their children's bent or set of strengths, skills, and interests and are ready to affirm them as they emerge. Ineffective parents often expect their children to be just like them or fulfill their unfulfilled dreams. Effective parents have a personal "mission statement" and a "family mission statement." They see parenting as a commitment for the long haul. Ineffective parents live from minute to minute often swept along by circumstances.	Proverbs 22:6—"Train up a child in the way he should go, and when he is old he will not turn from it." Have you ever tried to train someone without an "end in mind?" It's difficult. Teachers have lesson plans and builders have architectural plans. What's your plan for training your child?
3. Put first things first. We must learn to pursue our priorities by avoiding the tyranny of the urgent. The priorities for our life are part of our personal and family mission statements.	Effective Christian parents know that their children are "first things" in God's eyes. They put family at the head of any list. Ineffective parents are easily distracted and never seem to get around to doing those things that support God's best for them.	II Chronicles 1:11, 12—"Since this is your heart's desire and you have not asked for wealth, riches or honor, nor for the death of your enemies, and since you have not asked for a long life but for wisdom and knowledge to govern my people over whom I have made you king, therefore wisdom and knowledge will be given you." Solomon put first things first and God honored his decisions.

---

* From *The Seven Habits of Highly Effective People* (New York: Simon and Schuster, 1989).

Continued

Habits of Effective Christian Parents (continued)

4. Think win/win. Win/win is a frame of mind and heart that constantly seeks mutual benefit in all human interactions. One of us doesn't always have to lose.

Effective Christian parents try to maintain a relational balance with their children. Instead of fighting over every little thing, they try to see if God's way might emerge from discussion and dialog. Ineffective parents can't bear the thought of ever admitting they are wrong.

Colossians 3:21—"Fathers, do not embitter your children or they will become discouraged." The King James Version says, "Provoke not your children to anger." Provoking is often a result of entering into a relationship with the idea that I have to win and my kids have to lose. That's sin. God wants us to empower our children to become the young men and women He wants them to be.

5. Seek first to understand . . . then be understood. Listening is the activity of the heart. We need to learn to listen for understanding. We do a great service to others when we help them to clarify what it is that they just said.

Effective Christian parents try not to assume they know what their child is thinking or doing. They listen for understanding before speaking. How many people have gotten into trouble because they have assumed that what someone has said is exactly what they meant? Many home squabbles escalate because neither parent nor child takes the time to clarify what was being said.

James 1:19—"Everyone should be quick to listen, slow to speak and slow to become angry." Proverbs 10:19—"When words are many, sin is not absent, but he who holds his tongue is wise."

6. Synergy. Value differences. The whole is greater than the sum of its parts. See if we can make our differences complement each other instead of tear us apart.

Effective Christian parents know that something beautiful happens when the family is pulling together. Ineffective parents are interested in personal control even at the expense of "family body life."

I Corinthians 12:12—"The body is a unit, though it is made up of many parts; and though all its parts are many, they form one body." Do you see your family as being a part of the body of Christ? As Christians it is. Everyone in your home contributes something unique. Ineffective parents don't want to acknowledge that they could learn from their children.

7. Sharpen the saw. Preserving and enhancing "you." It's renewing yourself physically, mentally, socially, emotionally, and spiritually.

Effective Christian parents know that they need to take care of themselves. The starting point is daily time with the Lord. Ineffective parents fear change and improvement. They especially fear "growing in the Lord" because of what it might mean for their lives.

I Thessalonians 5:23—"May God himself, the God of peace, sanctify you through and through. May your whole spirit, soul and body be kept blameless at the coming of our Lord Jesus Christ." Some parents belittle the value of taking care of themselves. Other parents pamper themselves at the expense of their children. God wants balance as we exercise our spiritual, physical, social, and emotional muscles so we can stay fit.

Effective Parenting Evaluation

RS-9C

Read through the following statements, placing an "X" on the scale to indicate the degree to which each statement represents you. When you have finished, write a short-term goal statement indicating how you might strengthen those areas where your score was low.

	Needs Work						That's Me!

- My kids would say I'm a good listener. They often ask me to listen to their thoughts and concerns.

  1   2   3   4   5   6   7

- I have a plan for my life based on my understanding of God's Word and God's best for my life.

  1   2   3   4   5   6   7

- I have sat down and prayerfully considered what it is I feel God wants me to build into my child's life.

  1   2   3   4   5   6   7

- I am seldom the victim of my moods and circumstances.

  1   2   3   4   5   6   7

- I don't blame others for what happens to me.

  1   2   3   4   5   6   7

- I really believe that my children are gifts from God.

  1   2   3   4   5   6   7

- I take care of myself spiritually.

  1   2   3   4   5   6   7

- I take care of myself physically.

  1   2   3   4   5   6   7

- I take care of myself socially.

  1   2   3   4   5   6   7

- I take care of myself emotionally.

  1   2   3   4   5   6   7

- I respect the different viewpoints my children bring to the family.

  1   2   3   4   5   6   7

- I feel that our family is moving forward together.

  1   2   3   4   5   6   7

- I seldom find myself dealing with urgent matters and ignoring the truly important things in my life.

  1   2   3   4   5   6   7

- My spouse and I share the same parenting goals.

  1   2   3   4   5   6   7
  Needs Work   That's Me!

To strengthen areas of weak parenting habits, in the next week I will . . .

The Dirty Dozen

Parenting Strategies for an Unhappy Family

1. Do your own thing whenever you want to. Don't take into account the needs of your children. No matter what it is you want to do, you owe it to yourself to do it.

2. Make sure any disagreement turns into a war. Let your children know who's boss. Prepare them for the real world.

3. Let your children know that you are always right. Anything they say should be ridiculed, criticized, and corrected according to your view of the world.

4. Give your children no say in the rules you establish. Retain the right to break, ignore, and readjust these rules at any time.

5. Consider your children as imperfect, illogical, and unrealistic. It is your perception of reality that matters, not theirs.

6. Make your kids obey your word without question or explanation.

7. Treat your career and personal interests as more important than your children. Remember, it is quality time, not the quantity of time, that counts.

8. Don't worry about praying for your kids. Don't force your spiritual views on your children by taking them to Sunday school or church. They can make their own decisions when they get older.

9. When your kids blow it, hold a grudge. Remind them often that they have made a mistake. Keep a list of all past wrongs and be prepared to throw it at them whenever you feel they deserve it.

10. Don't try to understand what your children are going through. Remind them how tough it was when you were young. Compare them to kids who do better in school, athletics, and other pursuits.

11. To keep from worrying, don't keep track of where your kids are or what they are doing. You don't want to appear noisy. Besides, what you don't know won't hurt you.

12. Let the church and school teach your children right from wrong and how to make moral decisions. Feel free to rescue your kids from bad consequences of their choices.

Clarifying the Parenting Issues

Answer true or false to the following statements.

True False

_____ _____ 1. Kids want a relationship with their parents.

_____ _____ 2. Rules without relationship leads to rebellion.

_____ _____ 3. Times have changed so much. Everything my kid is going through is different than what I faced.

_____ _____ 4. Choose your battles wisely or you'll be battling all the time.

_____ _____ 5. Kids are impressed when you say "When I was your age. . . ."

_____ _____ 6. Kids will react better if they feel supported before being challenged.

_____ _____ 7. Kids are under so much pressure, they don't need an environment filled with consequences.

_____ _____ 8. Kids think faith is stupid.

_____ _____ 9. The world is such a scary place that parents need to be especially strict with their kids.

_____ _____ 10. The world is a scary place, so parents shouldn't add to it by making their kids afraid of them. Parents should avoid making any rules.

_____ _____ 11. Kids are more mature these days.

_____ _____ 12. This is a new day and age. Kids don't need a dad.

_____ _____ 13. It's impossible for a single parent to raise a healthy child these days.

_____ _____ 14. There are kids who need a "tougher" kind of love.

_____ _____ 15. It's okay to rescue children from their own mistakes.

> 1. I can do anything I please.
> 2. I am the boss.
> 3. I am always right.
> 4. Children have no say in setting rules.
> 5. My viewpoint is the only one that counts.
> 6. My word is final.

Consequences*

"Everything a parent needs to know about helping kids learn about privilege and responsibility."

EXCESSIVE CONTROL . . .

• Makes parents and teachers responsible for children's behavior.
• Prevents children from learning to make their own decisions.
• Prevents children from learning through decisions the rules for effective behavior.
• Suggests that acceptable behavior is expected only in the presence of authority figures who can enforce limits and expectations. It invites limit testing and continued negotiation of limits.
• Makes it easy for adults to be inconsistent (from guilt or fatigue).
• Creates an environment of rebellion and defiance.

NATURAL AND LOGICAL CONSEQUENCES . . .

• Hold children responsible for their own behavior.
• Allow children to make their own decisions about their actions and to experience the results.
• Teach children to experience a natural order of events.
• Teach that behavior has natural results rather than results based on the wishes of another person. It allows the child to feel powerful and secure in the outcome of events.
• Relieve adults of the frequent need to structure and restructure.
• Create less guilt and hostility in the parents resulting in a greater ability to express positive regard for the child.

PRINCIPLES FOR ESTABLISHING LOGICAL CONSEQUENCES

1. Consequences must be closely related to the positive or negative behavior.
2. Consequences must be reasonable to both adult and child.
3. Consequences should be stated in terms of privilege and responsibilities.
4. Consequences should be established prior to the event by mutual agreement of both child and adult.
5. Consequences should be established in an environment of unqualified love and mutual respect.
6. Consequences, once established, should have consistent follow-through.
7. Consequences should be enforced with dignity and respect.
8. When something unanticipated occurs, handle it as close to a natural consequence as possible, avoiding overkill and punitive responses. Then, if it's likely to be a problem in the future, agree on different consequences.
9. Family meetings provide excellent opportunities for children to be involved in decisions regarding consequences.

---

* Adapted from Stephen Glenn, Participant's Workbook, *Developing Capable People Manual* (Provo, Utah: Sunrise, Inc., 1991), pp. 7.14, 7.17. Used with permission.

What I Want to Build into My Child

Pretend it is your ninetieth birthday. You still are quite active. You walk into your home after your morning round of tennis and "Surprise!" Your children and close friends have thrown you a birthday party. During the course of the party your children get up to talk about the impact your life has had on theirs. What would you want them to say?

I. Write a six-sentence speech you'd like one of your children to give about you.

II. If these are the things I want my children to say about me, I need to be building these qualities into their lives now.

1. What personality characteristics would I like them to be noted for?

2. What perceptions about themselves do I want them to hold?

3. What core values and beliefs would I like them to cherish?

4. What skills do I think my children will need?

5. How do I plan on teaching them?

Parenting Strategies

✂ —

1. You try to nurture an internal control in your child so that he or she is not dependent on adults to make wise decisions.

✂ —

2. You are teaching your child about life by modeling good decision making in the way you communicate.

✂ —

3. You have a long-term relationship with your child. It's obvious there is a pattern of good communication.

✂ —

4. Your child is encouraged to assess the situation and respond to what he or she sees taking place. You ask your child to think about other possible behaviors than the chosen one.

✂ —

5. You work to create an environment of love in your home. If necessary, you are willing to use a "tough love" kind of approach to get your child's attention.

✂ —

6. Your child is encouraged to learn from what has happened.

✂ —

7. You work hard at trying to develop a firm, yet, relationally consistent environment. You consistently model good communication.

✂ —

8. You try to stay calm no matter what "button is pushed." There is no yelling, screaming, intimidating, manipulating, crying, or gnashing of teeth. You don't try to teach when your feelings are too intense.

✂ —

9. You ask for your child's side of the story. You don't assume anything. Even though another adult has told his or her version of the story, you explore your child's perceptions of what happened.

✂ —

10. You listen. You seek to understand both content and feelings.

✂ —

11. You anticipate challenges and talk to your child about them ahead of time.

✂ —

12. You pray regularly for your child. You aren't afraid to call on the Lord in times of trouble.

✂ —

13. You don't tell your child how to respond. You explore with your child what has happened, why it happened, the consequences, and how a negative situation might be avoided in the future. The child learns through the interaction while you show respect for the other adults involved in the child's life.

✂ —

Continued

14. Your child is able to identify feelings, pinpoint what triggered them, and then analyze what and why certain things were happening.

15. It's obvious that you as the parent have an "goal" in mind for your child, a plan for what you want to build into his or her life. You know how to work that plan.

16. You are willing to bring in other persons to help. You don't try to make your child feel any worse than he or she actually feels.

17. You have established a consequential environment in the home. As much as possible, the consequences flow naturally from the child's actions.

18. Your interaction focuses in on your child and his or her actions, not the behavior of others. Your child cannot control what other people do.

19. The principles in your home are based on spiritual roots and values.

20. You don't let your child off the hook nor do you allow the hook to be set too deeply.

21. As a parent, you aren't overly permissive. Thus, your child isn't able to explain his or her actions away by blaming others. You don't rescue your child from the consequences.

22. You aren't overly strict. You are balanced in your approach to your child. Your child will pay the consequences but he or she won't be thrown into a "locked cell."

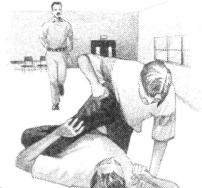

Setting: Randy's room

Parent *(entering room)*: Randy, do you have a minute? I need to talk with you.

Randy *(seated on bed with earphones on)*: Not right now. I'm busy.

Parent: Randy, I really need to talk with you now *(sits on bed)*.

Randy: All right, what do you want?

Parent: Randy, I received a call from your principal this afternoon. Do you have any idea what it might be about?

Randy: Yeah . . . it was the fight at lunchtime, wasn't it? But it wasn't my fault. It just happened.

Parent: I heard what the principal, Mrs. Mitchell, had to say. Now I want to hear about it from your perspective.

Randy: Mrs. Mitchell must really hate me.

Parent: No, she's disappointed in the way you responded to the situation. But she doesn't hate you. Now, tell me what happened.

Randy: Well, I was eating lunch with my friends when those guys you think are gangbangers came by the table and started messin' with us. I know we've talked about how to act around guys like that, but I just kinda lost it.

Parent: Messin' with you?

Randy: Yeah, you know. They started grabbing our food and throwin' it around.

Parent: Go on.

Randy: Then, they grabbed my homework—the stuff I worked on all weekend—and threw it around the room. I was so angry.

Parent: So, when you got angry what went through your head?

Randy: I remembered what you taught me about not losing my temper when I get angry. I tried to think of some better ways of dealing with it. But . . . I got so mad that I grabbed Tony and punched him.

Parent: What happened then?

Randy: When he fell down, I jumped on him. I was going to hit him again, but a security guard ran over and pulled me off.

Parent: After that . . . ?

Randy: I don't know exactly. The guard took me to the principal's office. I heard some of the other guys got into a big fight after that. It was pretty awful. What did Mrs. Mitchell say?

Parent: Your story is in line with what was reported to her. How are you feeling now?

Randy: Not real good. My hand hurts . . . that boy's got a hard head! And I've got the feeling I'm in trouble. Tony and those guys will be out to get me now. I'm afraid of what they might do to me.

Parent: Randy, this isn't the first time this year this has happened.

Randy: I know. I'm trying! But it's so hard.

Parent: Randy, I'm disappointed that you chose the response you did. What could you have done differently?

Randy: I dunno. They were being real jerks. It would have been impossible to ignore them. But . . . I guess I could have gone over to one of the security people and asked for help or just gotten up and left.

Parent: Why didn't you do that?

Randy: Well, I didn't want to look like I was some kind of weakling! Telling an adult is like admitting I can't handle things. It was just real confusing. Everything happened so fast.

Parent: Well, I can understand the confusion, especially in the midst of a situation like that. But, Randy, if those boys were gangbangers, who knows what could have happened! Haven't we talked about how to get out of situations like that? There had to be a better way of dealing with it.

Randy: I know. But talking about it at home is different than when you're dealing with it right then in school. It was really hard. Man, if those guys weren't such jerks I wouldn't be in such trouble!

Continued

Parent: I agree, they acted like jerks. But you know what we've always said "The only—"

Randy: I know, I know. "The only person you can control in a relationship is you."

Parent: Well, think about it a bit more. Because you know you're going to be faced with situations like that in the future at your school. You've got to choose better. Now, what do you think are the consequences of all this?

Randy: Besides having a sore hand and being afraid to see those guys again? Well, Mrs. Mitchell told me I'm suspended for a week.

Parent: That's right. You will be held responsible, though, for all your school work for every day during the suspension.

Randy: Oh, man.

Parent: It also means you won't be eligible to play basketball during the suspension.

Randy: What? That's not fair! The league playoffs are next week. I can't miss the playoffs. The team needs me.

Parent: Did coach lay out the rules for participation early in the year?

Randy: Well, yeah . . .

Parent: I know you weren't even thinking about it, but you did understand the rules?

Randy: Yes, but I . . . this is bogus!

Parent: Randy, you knew the rules. You knew what the consequences were. By choosing to fight . . . you pay the consequences.

Randy: But it's not fair.

Parent: It might not seem fair to you but who made the choice to fight? *(Silence for a few moments.)* Randy, whose choice was it?

Randy: Well . . . mine. But I wasn't thinking.

Parent: I know. It's really hard. But do you remember what I've taught you about making decisions?

Randy: Yeah . . . that it's best to do what Jesus would do.

Parent: That's right. What would Jesus want you to do to clean up this situation?

Randy: Oh, come on! I don't want to apologize to Tony.

Parent: I know you don't, Son, but it seems to me that if you're old enough to behave yourself into a situation, you're big enough to try to make it right again.

Randy: All right. I'll apologize.

Parent: When?

Randy: I'll call tonight.

Parent: How are you feeling right now?

Randy: I don't know. I guess I feel angry at myself because I chose what I knew was wrong. And I'm real sad because I'm going to miss some big games and I'm worried that people are going to be mad at me for a while. I'm mad at Tony and those guys he hangs out with for being jerks and putting me in this situation in the first place.

Parent: This has happened before, Randy. What do you think you can do to make sure it doesn't happen again?

Randy: I don't know.

Parent: I want you think about it some more. You do seem to do some irrational things when you get angry. You need to think it through a bit more. We're not done talking about all of this. I love you but I want you to know that I am disappointed in your decisions today.

Randy: Is that all?

Parent: No, there's one more thing. Do you remember what happened to your brother?

Randy: He got in big trouble. You had to call the police on him.

Parent: Do you know why?

Randy: I guess 'cause he never wanted to follow the rules. He was a real jerk about everything.

Parent: That's right. Randy. That was the toughest thing I've ever done. He just wouldn't work with us here. We finally had to force him to accept some pretty major consequences. Randy, I'll be as tough on you as you need. But I don't want to be all that tough. If you need someone else to talk to, I'd be glad to call Mike at the church and see if he would spend some time with you.

Randy: No, that's okay.

Parent: Okay, then. Would you mind if we prayed about this situation now? I want to make sure we get God's help on all this.

Street Smarts for Kids

The following questions have been suggested by the Sheriff's Office of Cook County, Illinois. Answer "yes" or "no" for each one, using a different mark (check, X, star, etc.) for each child. To help your children avoid violence, review these questions with them.

Yes	No	
___	___	1. Do your children know their full names, addresses, and phone numbers?
___	___	2. Do they know how to make an emergency phone call?
___	___	3. Have you ever walked the neighborhood with your children, pointing out areas of concern and safe places they can go in case of danger?
___	___	4. Do your children know they should never accept gifts or rides from strangers?
___	___	5. Have you taught them to memorize or write down the license number and description of any car of an adult who offers them a ride?
___	___	6. Have you taught your children to go to a store clerk or security guard to ask for help if they feel threatened in any way?
___	___	7. Do your children know it's okay to say NO to an adult (even someone they know) who wants to touch them in a way that would make your child feel uncomfortable?
___	___	8. Do your children know the safest route to go to school?
___	___	9. Have you impressed on your children the need to play with friends in open areas?
___	___	10. Do your children know to keep the house key hidden in a safe place so that no one knows that an adult won't be at home when your child gets home from school?
___	___	11. Do your children know that they should walk confidently and be alert to what is going on around them?
___	___	12. Do your children feel a sense of responsibility for other children? Are they taught to be alert and to inform adults if another child is being threatened?
___	___	13. Do your children know how to reach you at all times?
___	___	14. Do your children have an adult in the neighborhood they would feel comfortable talking to in case of danger?
___	___	15. Have you worked out an escape plan in case of fire?
___	___	16. Do your children know never to open the door to a stranger when they are alone in the house or apartment?
___	___	17. Have you alerted your children to the danger of answering the phone and accidentally letting a stranger know they are alone?
___	___	18. Do your children know how to lock doors and windows?
___	___	19. Have you taught your children to run away from any stranger who makes inappropriate advances?
___	___	20. Do they know that they should run away, screaming, making lots of noise? Do they know that it is important to run to the nearest place where there are lots of people?

Gang Information Sheet

Information provided by the Sheriff's Office of Cook County, Illinois.

TRENDS
- The emergence of gangs in communities where they have never been seen before including small and mid-size communities far removed from major metropolitan areas.
- The direct relationship between drug trafficking and gangs.
- The direct correlation between gangs and lethal violence.

DEFINITION
- A gang is a cohesive group of youth, usually between the ages of eleven and twenty-three, who have recognizable leadership, a purpose, and various levels of membership. Factors that distinguish the gang from other youth groups include a consistent use of violence, involvement in multiple criminal activities, a designated turf, and a pathological need for recognition.

GANG BEHAVIOR
- Conflict, vandalism, substance abuse and trafficking, hanging out, recruitment, subgroup formation relative to age (senior members to peewees), planned as well as spontaneous negative activities, nonconformity with legitimate systems, identification through graffiti, gang names, colors, hand signs, terminology, clothing, jewelry, and neighborhood boundaries.

COMMONLY CITED REASONS FOR YOUTH GANG INVOLVEMENT
- Need for identity/status/recognition/security, negative peer pressure, sense of control over one's immediate environment, low impulse control, to achieve a sense of power, perceived need for self-protection and survival, lack of positive use of idle time, lack of positive social and recreational opportunities, and a sense of intrigue and excitement associated with the gang.

GENERAL TIPS
- Understand the causes of gang development, do not glorify gangs by printing their names in newspapers, etc., remove graffiti immediately after taking a photo of it, know your neighborhood (people and events), network with other parents, know where kids hang out and what they are doing.

Continued

PARENT TIPS

- Talk with your child about life away from home.
- Recognize that kids know what is going on.
- Teach your kids about gangs at an early age (don't wait for the gangs to teach them).
- Notice how your child dresses (colors, hats, laces). Contact your local law enforcement officials for information on the characteristics and indications of the specific area gangs.
- Notice sudden changes in attitudes, friends, and language.
- Watch for unusual drawings on your kids' books, papers, or clothing.
- Make your child understand that you have no tolerance for gang behavior of any kind.
- If there is a gang problem in your area, mobilize to counteract it.
- If you have concerns, ask someone who is knowledgeable.

The following ideas were provided by Dan Korem, Streetwise Parents—Foolproof Kids *(Downers Grove, Ill.: NavPress, 1992), pp. 216, 217, 225, 226.*

Why Kids Disengage from a Gang

1. Youth simply lose interest as they get older.

2. The gang activity doesn't satisfy their expectations for a mask or distraction or give them power over their pain, and they realize that what the gang promises is an illusion.

3. They become frightened by the gang's activities.

4. They become frightened by some associated activity. For example, youth who join a gang to have a caring "family" sometimes get out if they become terrified of an external danger, such as drug dealers who threaten the gang.

5. It is successfully pointed out that their pain and their fear of pain is being exploited by the gang leaders. Gang members don't like to believe that anyone or anything can manipulate them or have control over them.

6. They discover that they fit a predictable profile—that is, gang members have certain expectations, behavior, etc.—causing them to realize they aren't that "unique."

7. Family relationships are restored and their familial problems are addressed.

8. Someone helps them find a solution to successfully deal with the source of their pain or problem.

"Deliver Us from Evil"

RS-13C

Read aloud the bold-faced lines. Your leader will respond with the lines in normal print.

Love must be sincere.

And I call you to love even those you hate. How many violent people have never felt a sincere love?

Hate what is evil.

There is so much evil we just accept and do nothing about.

Be devoted to one another in brotherly love.

There is power in the unity of Christian love.

Honor one another above yourselves.

We have to be there for one another. It's too difficult to be alone.

Never be lacking in zeal, but keep your spiritual fervor.

How can we go to battle against violence with a wishy-washy faith?

Be joyful in hope.

Jesus said that He would never leave or forsake us. With Him by our side we needn't lack hope.

Be patient in affliction.

All things work towards the good for those who love the Lord even when we don't understand God's timing.

Be faithful in prayer.

It is your greatest weapon as a parent.

Share with God's people who are in need.

Look around this room. Someone is hurting. An old African proverb says, "It takes a whole village to raise a child." It takes a whole church to raise a child these days.

Practice hospitality.

Your home could be the warmth that another family needs.

Bless those who persecute you.

Trying to counteract a violent world will make you enemies. Will you be willing to bless them in the midst of your frustration with them?

Bless and do not curse.

Cursing is a violent act that requires no courage.

Rejoice with those who rejoice.

May their joy be yours.

Mourn with those who mourn.

In a violent world, you will need to learn this. Is the church the place where mourners find comfort?

Continued

Live in harmony with one another.

When the body is united, we can make a difference for the sake of our children.

Do not be proud.

Pride gets in the way of using our gifts and talents to serve our God.

Be willing to associate with people of low position.

Those who have been given much are required to give much. Perhaps you can be the answer to another's prayer.

Do not be conceited.

There is enough in this world that will humble you.

Do not repay anyone evil for evil.

Violence begets violence.

Be careful to do what is right in the eyes of God.

We are called to live holy and blameless lives.

Live at peace with everyone.

Blessed are the peacemakers.

Do not take revenge.

The cycle becomes so vicious.

It is mine to avenge, I will repay, says the Lord.

God knows. There is a judgment. There is a just God.

If your enemy is hungry, feed him or her.

Perhaps the food you give will give the person strength to start a different kind of journey.

If someone is thirsty, give that person something to drink.

It might change a life.

Do not be overcome by evil.

God is Lord over all. He is King. Keep your eyes focused on Him.

Overcome evil with good.

Go, make disciples . . . loving those you encounter in the name of the Lord . . . make a difference in the life of your healthy child, in your community. . . . You can raise kids in a violent culture. . . . If you don't, who will?